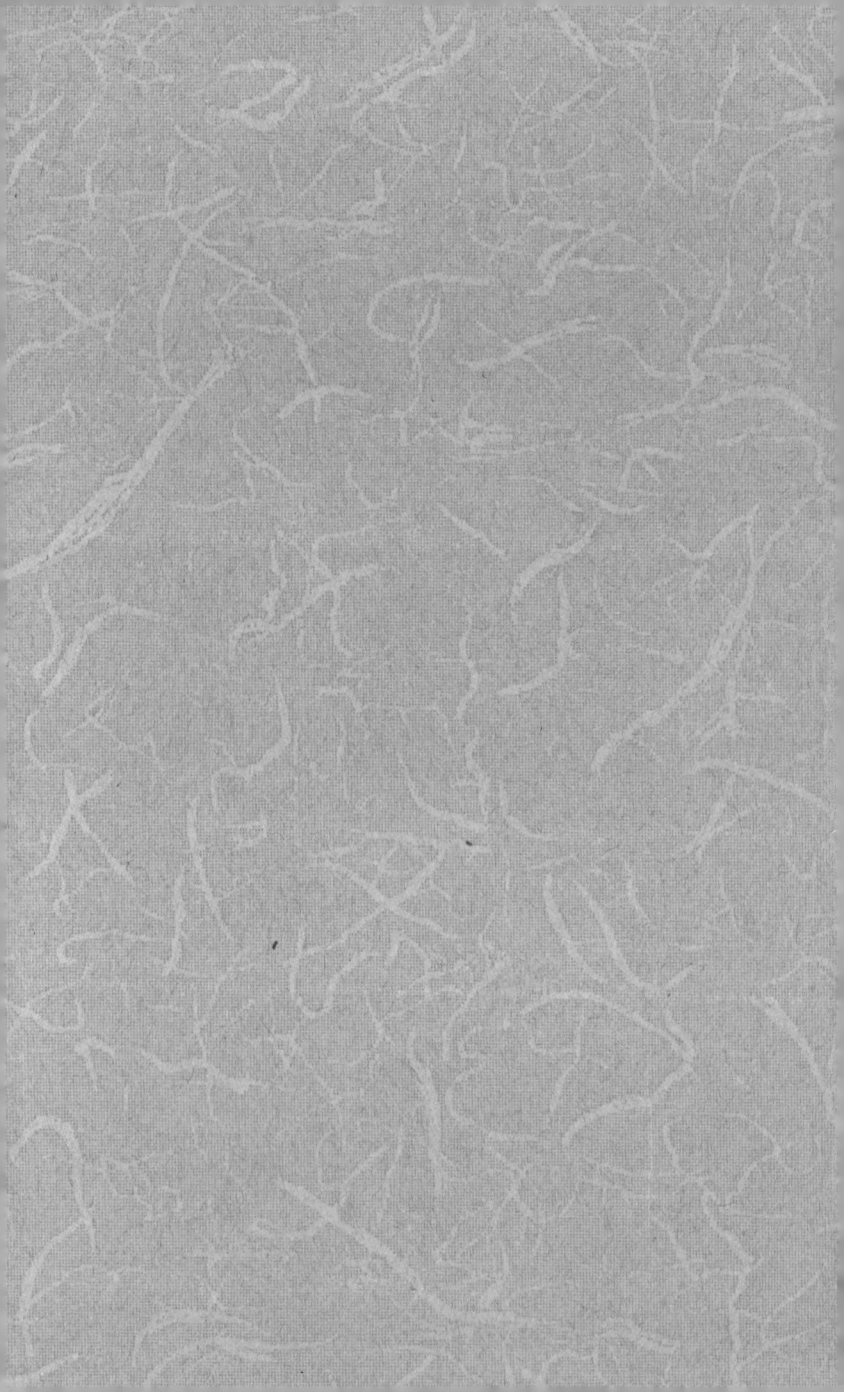

Some Final Words of Advice

The publisher gratefully acknowledges
the generous contribution
of Mr. Günther Klinge
to the publication of this volume.

Saikaku Ihara

Some Final Words of Advice

translated, and with an introduction by Peter Nosco

Charles E. Tuttle Company
Rutland, Vermont and Tokyo, Japan

REPRESENTATIVES

For Continental Europe:
BOXERBOOKS, INC., *Zurich*

For the British Isles:
PRENTICE-HALL INTERNATIONAL, INC., *London*

For Australasia:
BOOK WISE (AUSTRALIA) PTY. LTD
104–108 Sussex Street, Sydney 2000

This translation has received an award from the Translation Center at Columbia University, made possible by a grant from the National Endowment for the Arts.

Published by the Charles E. Tuttle Company, Inc.
of Rutland, Vermont & Tokyo, Japan
with editorial offices at
Suido 1-chome, 2–6, Bunkyo-ku, Tokyo

Copyright in Japan, 1980
by Charles E. Tuttle Co., Inc.

All rights reserved

Library of Congress Catalog Card No. 78–66086
International Standard Book No. 0–8048 1249–7

First printing, 1980

PRINTED IN JAPAN

To the memory of
Ivan Morris
1925–76

◆ ◆ ◆ Table of Contents

TRANSLATOR'S INTRODUCTION	9
Part One : Some Reflections on Japanese Townsmen	29
COMPILER'S PREFACE	31
1 · *The Village Called "Wayside" in Settsu Province*	33
2 · *Secrets of Turning Mushrooms into Money*	45
3 · *From Old Account Books to Eighteen Employees*	56
4 · *Omi Province, Mosquito Nets, a Clever Woman*	66
5 · *The Hozu River and a Millionaire from Yamazaki*	76
6 · *A Mother-in-law's Instructions after the Honeymoon*	86
7 · *A Modern-day Kusunoki Masashige*	99
8 · *Mr. Happiness, the Salt Vendor*	103
9 · *Something Popular and in Style*	111

Part Two : People's Hearts in This World of Ours   115

AUTHOR'S PREFACE   117

10 · *Reeling in a Compliant Old Badger*   118
11 · *The Arts and What They Can Do to People*   125
12 · *Second Thoughts about Passions*   133
13 · *The Traveling Salesman Who Sold Advice*   142
14 · *The Bridge of the Landlady's Nose*   148
15 · *A Bill Collector's Life . . . and Death*   157
16 · *Ise—Where They Know You at a Glance*   168
17 · *The Buddha Box That No One Saw for Free*   180
18 · *Spending a Day at the Employment Agency*   189
19 · *A Pawn Ticket for a Set of Armor, with Headpiece*   200
20 · *A Lady's Change of Heart*   209
21 · *A Few Words on Servants*   216
22 · *A Parent's Love for His Child*   225
23 · *Some Advice for When You Make Your Fortune*   230

SUGGESTIONS FOR FURTHER READING   239

♦ ♦ ♦ Translator's Introduction

While it is virtually a commonplace that in every period of historical transition the elements of continuity will outweigh those of discontinuity, life in Japan in the seventeenth century was quite different from what it had been in preceding eras. A few changes had occurred, changes so significant that the very fabric of the society was changed in a myriad of ways, and among these changes certainly the greatest was that the land was once again at peace. After decades of uninterrupted warfare and upheaval, there emerged at least a semblance of a unified state. With its headquarters in Edo (modern Tokyo), the new government known as the Bakufu presided over the various domains which formed the Japanese islands, and at the top of this government sat the shogun. The politically impotent emperor, based with his circle of courtiers and ancient nobility in the capital city, Kyoto, carried on much as Japanese emperors had done for centuries, surviving largely because of his extraordinary symbolic prestige and his performance of religious rites intimately associated with the well-being of the nation.

One immediate effect of this newfound peace was felt in the world of letters. It was as if the pent-up intellectual energies of the nation, restless after a long period of frustrated expression, had been suddenly released in a joyous, albeit somewhat chaotic, outburst of literary activity. Poetry, fiction, and the theater would all emerge with new modes and styles to match the new times. In the area of philosophy, the Bakufu, seeking to impose some sort of order upon this intellectual mélange, bestowed its patronage on a singular variety of Confucianism. This official Neo-Confucianism harbored a conspicuous distrust of feelings or human emotions for their ability to disrupt the delicate balance at the heart of the cosmos, and special emphasis was placed on correct human relations within the context of a rigid class system that placed samurai at the top followed by peasants, artisans, and merchants, in that order.

Despite the valiant efforts of the government to prop up this official ideology which was, in fact, little more than an intellectual rationalization for the particular system of rule endorsed by the Bakufu, the philosophy was under attack on a score of fronts by the close of the seventeenth century. Fortunately for both the society and the state, the basic assumptions of rule remained unchallenged. Most of the attacks were based instead on the issue of feelings and their importance in human relations. The notion that one's emotions were to be distrusted and even suppressed in order to appease the higher demands of integrity and righteousness was intellectually acceptable and yet ran counter to the nature and the instincts and the vitality of the society in which a Japanese of the seventeenth century operated. Furthermore, the assumption that peasants were near the top of the society and that merchants were at the bottom, while clearly an appreciation of the distinction between primary and secondary modes of production, could not survive long in an age when the merchant sector of society was growing in importance as rapidly as it was in Japan.

A historian might argue that political power resided in the rice-producing areas of the countryside, but no one would deny that excitement lay in the urban centers of Kyoto, Edo, and Osaka. For a citizen of those days, Kyoto brought to mind images of the ancient elegance of the imperial court. Edo was the administrative center of the nation, and despite the youth of the city in comparison with the stately dignity of the Capital, the city was clearly growing at a tremendous rate and few doubted that it was destined to eclipse its rival. But Osaka was a curious combination of elements from Kyoto and Edo and also had a number of features that were distinctly Osakan. Osaka had suffered badly during the wars of unification and as late as 1615 a final decisive battle had ravaged the city. Nonetheless, the residents moved with a characteristic swiftness to rebuild their ruins and to maintain their position as the economic center of the land. Contemporary accounts of Osaka give the impression of tremendous bustle with money and goods exchanging hands with such vigor and regularity that they formed the very pulse of the city. All three cities had at least one element in common—the consciousness of their residents that they constituted a new social group, which they themselves styled "the townsmen" *(chōnin)*.

The word "townsman" is one of those delightful words that seem purposely to elude strict definition. In its most limited sense, it implied the artisan or merchant or what we conveniently lump together under the label "businessman." However, samurai could also become townsmen if they no longer behaved like medieval warriors, as could clergymen and all other professionals as long as they made their homes in or near one of the major cities. To be a townsman, one did not need to be wealthy, nor did one need to be exceptionally urbane. In fact, literary sources suggest the only real requirement may have been a purely subjective one—that one think of the world as the Floating World.

We tend to think of the brilliantly colored woodblock prints when we hear the words Floating World, or *ukiyo* in Japanese, and the impression is not misleading. For a Japanese, the words were meant to bring to mind deeply ingrained and originally Buddhist notions of the transient and even illusory aspects of life. Translated into the hard terms of daily life, it meant living in a world where fortunes could be made overnight through a single fluctuation in the price of rice and where the mighty could just as easily and swiftly become the lowly—a world in which absolutely nothing was secure and in which the only solace and respite lay in those fleeting moments which were devoted to utterly sensual pleasures.

The world Ihara Saikaku* (1642–93) wrote about was the Floating World. Saikaku was a townsman born in the city of Osaka, and numerous critics both in Japan and

---

* Japanese names throughout this text, except on the title page and in the list of suggested readings, are given family name first.

elsewhere extol his works as second only to the great *Tale of Genji* in the long history of Japanese fiction. For an author of such repute, surprisingly little is known about his life. We do know that he was married and that his wife died when Saikaku was in his early thirties. We have reason to believe that he was fairly well-to-do, for after his wife's passing he seems to have devoted his life to travel and to his writings. Saikaku won his first literary acclaim, however, not as a novelist and short story writer, but rather as a writer of *haikai* verses.

Haikai verses were, originally, lighthearted verses which were linked together to form a prescribed sequence. The syllabic count, as in their more somber counterpart, the *waka*, was 5–7–5–7–7. When *haikai* verses were linked into longer compositions, the first poet would compose the first three lines (5–7–5), the second would compose the next two lines (7–7), and the third would compose the first three lines of the next poem, and so on until the sequence was brought to a close with a 7–7 couplet. The first verse of a linked-verse sequence was called the *hokku,* and during the seventeenth century it came to be regarded as a wholly independent verse; it was thus identical to the seventeen-syllable *haiku,* which was its immediate descendant.

Saikaku was the leading pupil of Nishiyama Soin (1605–82), the founder of the innovative Danrin school of verse, but Saikaku was not content simply to produce a *haikai* sequence of one hundred polished verses. He would compose *haikai* by the thousand!

In 1675 Saikaku made good his promise by composing one thousand verses in a single day at a rate of nearly two per minute. In 1677 he bettered his previous performance and produced one thousand six hundred verses in a twenty-four-hour period. What is astonishing is that he not only composed the poems but that he also transcribed them himself. As might have been expected, his performance brought on the challenges of other versifiers, and when freed from the task of doing his own transcriptions, Saikaku composed four thousand verses at the Sumiyoshi Shrine in Osaka in a single day and night. However, his all-time record occurred at the same site in 1684, when he recited an incredible twenty-three thousand five hundred verses, a rate of one verse every four seconds! This proved too fast even for the small army of copyists in attendance, who could do no more than simply mark their tally sheets.

However, if Saikaku had merely rested on his laurels as the champion of marathon *haikai* composition, it is inconceivable that he would be a major figure in the history of Japanese literature. The real breakthrough came in 1682 with the publication of his *Life of an Amorous Man,* which at once opened up an entirely new concept in Japanese fictional writing and also managed to spark the enthusiasm of a receptive reading public. The novel tells the story of Yonosuke, a Japanese cross between Don Juan and Robinson Crusoe, who has his first romantic adventure at the age of seven. Saikaku then traces Yonosuke's amorous career through the course of thousands of women and hundreds of men until at the age of sixty he retires from the world of active society and sets sail aboard a ship called the *S. S. Lust* bound for a mythical Isle of Women.

What made the work so outstanding was that it combined a classical elegance in vocabulary and style with themes addressed to the townsman in his contemporary setting. Yonosuke became a kind of Genji of the Floating World—a shining prince in this sensual realm—and the fifty-four chapters in the *Life of an Amorous Man,* identical to the number in the *Tale of Genji,* suggest that Saikaku consciously took the nearly seven-centuries-old masterpiece as his model. The newness of Saikaku's fictional prose thus, ironically, partook of this long-neglected novelistic form, while at the same time the themes were fresh because they were tailored to a new society.

Saikaku's style owed much to his training as a poet, and his terse, often epigrammatic prose cannot have been easy for his audience. Despite this, his style brilliantly combined elements of both the refined and the colloquial in a manner strikingly appropriate to the new genre for which he was responsible. Thanks to the development of commercial presses in the early seventeenth century, the book achieved considerable circulation and sold some one thousand copies in its first printing in Osaka alone. More importantly, however, it confirmed Saikaku in his career as a writer of fiction.

Saikaku produced his prose works at the same breathless pace which had earlier won him fame as a *haikai* poet. During the years 1685–88 he wrote full-length works on the average of one every three months, and this no doubt accounts for much of the uneven quality of his writing both from work to work and within individual works. Among the highlights of his writings in this period, one would have to list *Five Women Who Loved Love, The Life of an Amorous Woman, Tales of Samurai Duty,* and *The Japanese Family Storehouse.* Saikaku was the first truly popular writer of Japanese fiction, and it is interesting to speculate on just exactly who was doing so much reading during the closing years of the seventeenth century. Proceeding under the assumption that people then, as now, enjoyed reading about themselves, his works themselves provide us with the best clues.

Certainly the majority of those who were reading Saikaku during his lifetime were townsmen who lived in the cities, and probably the largest constituency was composed of merchants. Recent research on literacy rates immediately prior to the opening of Japan to the West in the nineteenth century suggests a conservative estimate of forty percent male literacy, higher, in fact, than anywhere else in the world at that time with the possible exceptions of England and Holland. Of course, more of those who could read lived in the cities than in the countryside, and thus it seems safe to imagine that most of those who made their livelihoods by trade in the market centers were literate and that many of them read works like those of Saikaku for their own amusement.

Likewise, many of the samurai probably found pleasure in reading Saikaku's accounts of their escapades. While this may at first sound surprising, it is useful to bear in mind that this hereditary class of warriors was turning to other pursuits in an age when their martial services were no longer required. Indeed, the government actively encouraged the transformation of the samurai into a class of literati.

A third group who may quite possibly have enjoyed Saikaku's more bawdy writings was precisely those courtesans who were such a favorite subject of his brush. Despite the official support of puritanical philosophies and social doctrines, the Bakufu licensed certain quarters in all the principal cities where prostitution and virtually every other imaginable form of sensual indulgence were allowed to flourish. The government may have been more interested in confining these activities to certain limited areas but it certainly was not blind to the opportunities for securing revenue from an otherwise uncontrollable phenomenon. In any case, it is not unreasonable to imagine that those who lived within the licensed quarters and made their trade out of entertainment found their own amusement in reading Saikaku. When he describes the plight of an impoverished courtesan who resorts to pawning her love letters (Chapter 19: "A Pawn Ticket for a Set of Armor, with Headpiece"), it does not ring false that she could have written the letters herself; and if she could write, then she could surely read as well.

Some Final Words of Advice (Saikaku Oritome) is one of a number of works by Saikaku which were published posthumously. Our only clue as to when the book was written appears in the opening paragraph of Chapter 5, where Saikaku informs us that he is writing in the early spring of 1689. All that we know about how the stories came into the form we have derives from the preface of Hojo Dansui (1663–1711), Saikaku's disciple and the compiler of the work. Dansui tells us that the two portions of *Some Final Words of Advice,* namely "Some Reflections on Japanese Townsmen" and "People's Hearts in This World of Ours," were intended to form a trilogy with *The Japanese Family Storehouse* so that by reading them, merchants and craftsmen might "acquire an understanding of daily life and adopt these tales as ideals on which to model their own lives." *The Japanese Family Storehouse* had already been completed in 1688, but the other two manuscripts were unfinished at the time of Saikaku's death in 1693. Likening the situation to "hiding a jewel in a swamp," Dansui explained his sense of obligation both to his master's wishes and to the need of the public to see these works.

Saikaku's own cryptic explanation for the work is found in his preface to the second portion of the book, "People's Hearts in This World of Ours." Here he implies that his mind was so full of his observations of "people's follies" that he just *had* to write them down or suffer the consequences of silence. This is rather different from the didactic implications of Dansui, and there is no mention that Saikaku thought of this work as part of a trilogy. It is quite conceivable that Dansui invented the notion of the trilogy and included Saikaku's name in the Japanese title of the work with no other purpose in mind than to stimulate bookstore sales and thereby enhance his claim to being the sole repository of his deceased master's intentions.

As for the question of why the works remained unpublished in Saikaku's lifetime, the most popular explanation is that the author was suffering from failing eyesight in his declining years and was physically unable to carry through with his project. Both "Some Reflections on Japanese Townsmen," which includes nine stories, and "People's Hearts in This World of Ours," which has fourteen, are considerably shorter than Saikaku's standard length for a book, but when put together they are roughly identical in length to that of his other major works. Here again it is possible that the invisible hand of Dansui has entered into the picture; with a fixed conception of how long a "book" should be, he may have trimmed certain stories or discarded others altogether in his compilation of *Some Final Words of Advice*. Nevertheless, the work as we have it is indisputably a product of Saikaku's brush. Both the style and the themes belong to the master, and the overall effect of the stories is most satisfying, though the exact nature of the satisfaction may vary from reader to reader and may perhaps be aided by some words of explanation.

While it would be impossible to isolate a single chapter in *Some Final Words* as typical, there are several features that recur in many if not most of the stories. Saikaku generally begins a chapter with a didactic statement that is often couched in highly poetic terms. This didactic statement is usually followed by a general, anecdotal observation of his age, which in turn will lead into an anecdote which is specific as to time, place, and character. Then, once the anecdote has run its course, Saikaku will use the device of a connecting or linking word to make his transition to a succeeding anecdote which may be only peripherally, if at all, related to the first.

Sometimes Saikaku's anecdotes do reinforce the moral messages with which his chapters open, but just as often they do not. Moreover the messages are likely to be contradictory from one chapter to the next. In one instance Saikaku will enumerate the virtues requisite to the acquisition of great wealth—virtues such as industriousness and meticulousness—and elsewhere he will baldly assert that it is useless to try to make money unless one has capital at hand to start out with; he may even ridicule the overly cautious. In the very first chapter of this book Saikaku admonishes the merchant who endangers his fortune through speculation on markets and through extravagance in the licensed quarters, but the story he proceeds to tell is of a young man who makes his fortune cornering the rice market by using some confidential information overheard in a brothel. The story can hardly be cited as evidence of the harm that awaits you if you visit the licensed quarters or engage in speculative hoarding!

The point which Saikaku is making through this jumble of conflicting testimony is that there are no infallible lessons to be learned or formulas to be memorized for amassing great sums of money or for achieving happiness. In the episode just cited, Saikaku does demonstrate the value of seizing the opportunity, a theme which recurs in these stories, but elsewhere we see Saikaku's characters being perfectly alert, clever, or industrious, all to no avail, while their more fortunate colleagues in this exercise succeed entirely by accident.

The transitions in Saikaku's narrative from the didactic to the anecdotal, from the general to the specific, and from narration to direct quotation are examples of the way he exploited elements of his style and language. The Japanese which Saikaku wrote was sufficiently flexible as to allow for a single sentence to continue for pages with no mention of the subject until the very end, if it appeared at all. In the original the reader has the sensation of being carried along by the prose, and with this momentary suspension of disbelief the overall effect is to make the content all the more convincing. For example, there is nothing to indicate that the author has slipped into direct quotation aside from the grammatical particle *to* at the very end. Thus the reader knows where a quotation has ended, but often he cannot tell with any degree of certainty where that quotation began. Since English prose does not allow for sentences without subjects or quotations which end but do not begin, the effect in translation is somewhat more jarring. The stories were meant to be savored as a succession of momentary glimpses, and the modern reader, if he wishes to capture the mood of the original, should engage in the same willing sense of belief that must have been practiced by Saikaku's readers in the seventeenth century.

It has often been said that Saikaku's writings mark a turning point in the development of Japanese realism because of their vivid treatment of contemporary themes. For example, Japanese critics have been fond of pointing to *The Life of an Amorous Man* as Saikaku's most realistic piece, primarily because of all Saikaku's works it most closely resembles early European novels in form. However, this assertion can only bemuse the Western critic who is inclined to view the satyrlike Yonosuke as a classic example of parody, irrespective of the medium in which he travels. Western students of Saikaku, on the other hand, have found realism in works like *Five Women Who Loved Love*, where realistically portrayed feelings play such an important role, especially when they bring the characters into conflict with accepted social behavior. *Some Final Words of Advice* is also "realistic." Structurally and stylistically the work is classically Saikakuesque, but thematically it contains elements which differ from those in any of his previous works.

Part of the author's great genius lay in his ability to sketch an extraordinarily vivid picture of a character or an event with only a few words, and here again the comparison with woodblock prints of the period is apt. In his earlier works Saikaku maintained a considerable emotional distance from his characters, and this distance was in large part responsible for the effectiveness of his prose. In *Some Final*

Words of Advice, however, Saikaku's emotional distance sometimes breaks down and society ceases to be a mere backdrop for the plot. On the one hand we find Saikaku interacting with his characters, while on the other we see his characters interacting with their environment. Particularly in the first portion of the book, "Some Reflections on Japanese Townsmen," where Saikaku still keeps himself at arm's length, as it were, the vividness of his prose provokes the reader into taking sides either for or against his characters in a most uncanny way. But whenever Saikaku allows that separation between himself and his work to contract, the consequent interactions result in both a new dimension in his realism and a genuine moral ambivalence in the actions of his characters, for neither Saikaku nor his reader can remain an amused bystander any longer.

For the first time in Saikaku's writings we encounter a realistic treatment of the issue of evil, and it can hardly be accidental that most of the instances occur in the fourteen chapters composing the second part of the book, "People's Hearts in This World of Ours." To give just one example, Chapter 15 closes with an account of the last moments of a critically ill child who dies before his family's eyes. Just as the child is about to breathe his last, a bill collector arrives from the local store demanding payment on long-standing debts. When he is rebuffed by the child's father the bill collector retorts, "We never agreed that you needn't pay your bills if the boy should die!" During this exchange the child passes away, and in his fury the father stabs the intruder and then kills himself, and there the chapter ends. The effect, needless to say, is devastating, and the entire episode consumes less than one page!

Here Saikaku has moved from the didactic ambivalence of conflicting directive to the moral ambiguity of a violent action provoked by an almost inhuman lack of sensitivity. In the example just cited and in many other places in the book, there is a pervasive current of bitterness. It is the bitterness of an old man for whom those sardonic aspects of life which might once have been amusing are no longer so. Perhaps it can be traced to Saikaku's failing health and eyesight, but equally plausible is the notion that he was tired of simple truths and the society that encouraged them. There is a seriousness here that transcends the limits of parody, and when in Chapter 16 Saikaku states, "For the most part, people's hearts in this world of ours are all pretty much the same," we do not need to be reminded that this conclusion is a far from happy one.

It is tempting to seek comparisons between Saikaku's fiction and works in the literary traditions of England and continental Europe. Daniel Defoe (1660–1731) comes most immediately to mind, particularly with such works as *The Complete English Tradesman* or *The Compleat English Gentleman*. Defoe, like Saikaku, was a townsman. He was born and spent most of his life in London, which as the capital and commercial center of England was not unlike an Edo, Kyoto, and Osaka all rolled into one grand metropolis. Just as Saikaku drew his characters from the townsmen who were his neighbors in the Floating World, Defoe's major characters are almost without exception drawn from the new middle class which emerged in the early years of the eighteenth century. Most English historians place the birth of the modern business world in the final decades of the seventeenth century, and out of this new realm of trade and finance grew a new sort of man, the tradesman, whose mark upon his society was as dramatic as that of the townsman in Saikaku's Japan.

The history of commercial presses in England is longer than it is in Japan, but until Defoe's time most writers had to rely either upon their own financial resources or upon wealthy patrons to meet the costs of publication. Defoe broke this pattern, again like Saikaku, by addressing his fictional prose to the interests of the newly emergent literate sectors of his society. Moreover, the virtues that Defoe attributed to his tradesman would surely have sounded familiar to Saikaku. For Defoe, the tradesman was a resilient and thoroughly qualified individual, a "kind of phoenix, who rises out of his own ashes, and makes the ruin of his fortunes to be a firm foundation to build his recovery" (*The Complete English Tradesman*).

Defoe also cautioned this versatile fellow against the hazards of extravagance in sensual matters. A sentence such as "Tradesmen neglect their shop and business to follow the track of their vices and extravagances: some by taverns, others to the gaming houses . . ." could belong to either Defoe or Saikaku, and only its continuation, "others to balls and masquerades, plays, harlequins, and operas," betrays its source as the former. Both writers appear to have drawn extensively from their own personal experiences and observations, and both were concerned with the personal attributes that accompanied the acquisition of wealth. However, Saikaku was more concerned with those characteristics which might help one to acquire wealth, whereas Defoe was far more interested in the social trappings which would invariably accompany that wealth. For Defoe this involved primarily the transition to a "gentleman," a term that, roughly prior to the death of Queen Anne in 1714, designated a status only obtainable by birth. Defoe insisted that gentility was acquirable; if being a gentleman meant possessing both wealth and breeding, then trade could produce that wealth and a liberal education could produce that breeding. His "true-bred merchant" was a universal scholar whose gifts included not only all the conventional forms of knowledge that a liberal education could provide, but also all the other qualifications and savvy that could only be learned in the school of the marketplace. Defoe scorned the man who possessed only book knowledge as a "learned fool" who was definitely "no scholar."

Of Defoe's fictional prose, the work that provides the most interesting comparison with *Some Final Words of Advice* is *The Fortunate Mistress*. Defoe never finished this work, and it was published in its incomplete version in 1724. In this work Defoe also picked up the theme of evil as it revolved around his heroine, Roxana. It is generally speculated that Defoe could not bring himself to complete *The Fortunate Mistress* because the implications of Roxana's depravity were too much for him to bear. In this work, Defoe, like Saikaku, had lost the distance separating him from his characters, and it is curious that in both instances the issue of human evil should rise to the fore. In Defoe's case, it was to be the last major piece of fictional prose that he wrote. It has been suggested that Saikaku chose not to have the stories in *Some Final Words of Advice* published during his lifetime for reasons similar to Defoe's, although here the evidence is less conclusive.

Nonetheless, while the parallels between these two authors and their respective worlds are intriguing, one obviously need not have read Defoe to appreciate Saikaku. The stories in *Some Final Words of Advice* have their own distinctly compelling quality and fascination. As with all collections of short stories it is preferable to space their reading over a period of a few days or evenings. My own final words of advice before entering the Floating World of the pages ahead are that the reader look for himself in the stories, for that was Saikaku's primary intent.

The illustrations that accompany the text are from the original edition published in 1694. They are generally attributed to Makieshi Genzaburo, a student of Yoshida Hambei, but a degree of controversy surrounds this attribution.

The primary text used has been the one in Volume II of *Saikaku-shu* edited by Noma Koshin (*Nihon Koten Bungaku Taikei* series, no. 48). I have also benefited from Kaneko Takeo's *Saikaku Oritome Shinkai* (Tokyo, 1969), but where the two disagree, I have tended to favor Professor Noma's interpretations.

ON FESTIVALS AND CURRENCY

Among the townsmen of Saikaku's time, festivals were used to mark the year, and money was used to mark a man's position in life. Since references to both occur repeatedly in Saikaku's work, it would be advisable for his readers to have some understanding of these matters.

There were five major festivals:

1/1 (first day/first month) *New Year's Day,* which was celebrated with especially fine foods and sakè. It customarily included a visit to a shrine and other ceremonial acts such as the First Writing, the drawing of First Water, and so on.

3/3 *The Doll's Festival,* which particularly favored young ladies. Elaborate collections of dolls were put on display within the household, and this was often combined with excursions to view flower blossoms and other ventures into the countryside.

5/5 *The Boy's Festival,* during which houses were decorated, often in such a manner as to indicate the number of sons within the household.

7/7 *The Festival of All Souls (Obon),* during which the spirits of those departed from this world were believed to return briefly to those places where they once lived. Lanterns were hung to guide the spirits home. This festival was second in importance only to New Year's Day.

9/9 *The Chrysanthemum Festival,* which was celebrated with chrysanthemum wine and excursions to view the changing colors of autumn.

Shortly after he established the Tokugawa Bakufu, the shogun Ieyasu attempted to impose order upon the economic affairs of the newly united land by establishing gold and silver standards for a new currency system. In his sweeping currency reform of 1636, the third shogun, Iemitsu, added copper, thus creating a trimetallic standard.

Gold was used primarily in Edo, the seat of the Bakufu, while the Kansai region surrounding Osaka and Kyoto clung to its practice of using silver as the base for exchange.

Copper was used extensively in the countryside. The Bakufu also established national mints, and the silver mint, or Ginza, which it licensed in 1612 in Edo, lent its name to the fashionable shopping district in today's Tokyo.

The respective value of coins was determined by the following weight relationships: 1 *kan* = 1,000 *momme* = 10,000 *fun* = 100,000 *rin* = 132 oz.

Gold denominations were: 1 *oban* (wt. 43 *momme*) = 9 *koban* = 9 *ryo* = 36 *bu*.

Silver denominations were: 1 *kamme* (wt. 1 *kan*) = 23 *chokin*.

Copper denominations were: 1 *kammon* (wt. 1 *kan*) = 960 *mon*.

These represent the major denominations. One ounce of gold was exchanged for 12.4 ounces of silver or for 210 ounces of copper. Units of currency have, on occasion, been altered within this translation for comparative clarity.

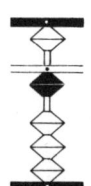 # Part One

Some Reflections on Japanese Townsmen

Part One

Some Reflections on Ignucius Trautman

◆ ◆ ◆ Compiler's Preface

The works of fiction produced during Saikaku's career are so numerous that there is scarcely a corner of the earth where they are not to be found. Among these stories, *The Japanese Family Storehouse*, *Some Reflections on Japanese Townsmen*, and *People's Hearts in This World of Ours* compose a work best known as the *Threefold Writings*. When merchants and craftsmen read these works, they acquire an understanding of daily life and adopt these tales as ideals on which to model their own lives.

When Saikaku died in the eighth month of the year 1693, *The Japanese Family Storehouse* had already been completed, but *Some Reflections on Japanese Townsmen* and *People's Hearts in This World of Ours* were left unfinished. It certainly cannot have been the author's intent that nothing but the names of these latter two works should have come down to us and that the *Threefold Writings* should remain incomplete. I even overheard someone in a bookstore lament that leaving the manuscripts to be taken over by bookworms was like hiding a jewel in a swamp. Accordingly, I have taken the remaining parts of these two works and joined them into one.

Saikaku had already finished his brief preface to this work, but when I recall how the Master died leaving his final accomplishment unfinished, I find myself dipping my brush into an inkstone already wet with tears.

—Dansui

1694

• 1 • The village called "wayside" in settsu province

Ever since the reign of the first emperor, Jimmu, there have been countless examples of men who, with their eyes blinded by passion, cavorted with beautiful women while their families fell into ruin. In recent times merchants have been stripped of their fortunes and driven into bankruptcy by two factors in particular—the first being lust, and the second, market speculation. Year after year the loss and senseless waste pile ever higher one atop the other: the blossoms of a merchant's flowering talents fall, his brocade robes are replaced by ones of paper, and finally, in the same way the seasons turn one to another, he is reduced to a faceless beggar. Consider all this and it should become apparent that for the merchant, in all his varied activities, there is simply no room for lack of heed.

Now in the town of Itami in Settsu Province, there was a family that began production of the finest quality Morohaku sakè and continued in this venture for generation upon generation. Yet when the accounts were set in order at the end of each year, there was never more or less than a scant five *kamme* of silver profit. The head of this family was said to be endowed with but small stature and an equally petty destiny, but as the days and months passed and his children grew into adults, his eldest son proved to be quite clever in any variety of matters. He abandoned the old ways of his parents and took to adorning himself in vestments of only the most fashionable cut and pattern, and from this he graduated to reveling in the company of prostitutes.

Time and again he stole away from his old village by night and dashed off to the Capital. There, in the licensed quarters known as Shimabara, he whittled away at his small fortune until but little remained. With their son's livelihood thus endangered, his parents lamented his fate. But, alas, it was to no avail, for he persisted undaunted.

On one occasion, through the good offices of a certain Shichizaemon of the Maruya house of assignation, he contracted to summon a *tayu* courtesan* named Yoshino for a rendezvous. With teams of bearers to speed his palanquin, he rushed most eagerly up to the Capital, arriving at the Tamba Gate just as the midnight bell was tolling. After restlessly pacing about, he heard the two A.M. curfew announced; and soon after, the gate opened to allow nocturnal pleasure seekers to wend their way home. The patrons, who had been entertaining their fanciful dreams since the early night hours, now sang melancholy tunes before finally turning away—"Oh, the bittersweet parting at narrow Shujaku Lane!"

At last his time had come, and upon seeing the lovely face of the awaiting courtesan his heart filled all the more with

---

* A courtesan of the highest rank.

No sooner had he stepped inside the Maruya house than he began giving orders. "First of all, bring me a washbowl and some rice soup!" he bellowed. "I want miso and white bread boiled in sakè, and a bowl of oysters as well. Bring a hibachi into the parlor right away for some of your cedar-grilled wild duck!"

thoughts of love. No sooner had he stepped inside the Maruya house than he began giving orders. "First of all, bring me a washbowl and some rice soup!" he bellowed. "I want *miso* and white bread boiled in sakè, and a bowl of oysters as well. Bring a *hibachi* into the parlor right away for some of your cedar-grilled wild duck!"

Smoke began to billow from the kitchen as everyone scurried about in haste to serve him. While the proprietor set up the *kotatsu* footwarmer, his wife prepared some dark tea and offered it, murmuring, "For your pleasure, sir." The eldest son had an assistant courtesan smooth his ruffled hair, bade another to stroke the soles of his feet, and for Yoshino he saved the task of massaging and stretching his fingers, gently, one by one. To the accompaniment of a sentimental ballad sung elsewhere in the house, he set himself to imbibing without further ado.

"Not even a daimyo could afford splendor like this," he boasted. "What I would really like to do is give you all such generous tips that the next time my voice is heard in this part of town, the jesters and entertainers and even those people at the seventeen tea houses by the entrance to Shimabara will jump out of bed in the middle of the frostiest night and happily cry out, 'He's back in town!' Anyway, what people really like is money. Why, if I were just to throw away my money without keeping track of it, there would be no limit to the fun we could have tonight. That Paradise people talk about is right here before your very eyes. But as they say, 'Everyone's a Buddha while he's asleep. . . .'"

With those words he dreamily stretched out alongside Yoshino on the *futon* bedding piled three-high for his comfort. Just as he was settling down to the evening's business, however, the front door of the house suddenly burst open.

Through the thin walls he could hear a runner delivering a message to one of the guests in the next room.

"Sir, a letter has come from your home."

"What could it be?" said the guest. "Ah, it looks like good news—word from one of my agents in Edo of some inside information that is sure to make me some quick money. All of the Kanto region has been hit by a typhoon, and the market price of rice there has gone right through the ceiling. So if I head down to Osaka to corner the market on rice from the Western Provinces and make a profit on the inflated prices, then I can buy out the contract on one of these courtesans and make her my wife.

"Pray for my good luck in this," he continued. "I'll set out as soon as it's light." Loath to leave his courtesan after so short a time, he was quite unable to tear himself from her side.

The young man from Itami perked up upon overhearing this news. He rose from the bedding, though as yet he had not so much as untied his sash, and abandoned all thoughts of the good time he might have enjoyed had the evening been allowed to reach its most interesting and absorbing point. "I've forgotten something back at home," he said, and paying no heed to the courtesan he took his leave. He rushed by carriage down to the docks, where he hired a skiff out of Fushimi, and by ten A.M. of that very day he reached the banks of the Yodo River in Osaka. Secretly he made his negotiations with a wholesaler, and from noon on, after he had cornered a good part of the rice supply, the price began to climb. Within just two hours he turned a profit of thirty-eight *kamme*. In the same way he cornered the oil market and made another forty-four *kamme* profit. He returned to Itami in the best of spirits.

When he showed his parents the veritable mountain of

koban coins that he had earned, they agreed that in an age when money was so hard to come by, this was proof indeed that he had the heart for becoming a millionaire. In due course he forgot all about those ladies whom he had so often visited up at the Capital and concentrated all his energies on the single task of making his livelihood as profitable as possible. This, of course, is the first step one takes on the road to great wealth.

He tried his hand at selling sakè in Edo, at lending money, and at real estate speculation. He built a splendid house for himself, and there he spent many happy springtimes. Whenever he celebrated the New Year with his family, his father donned an apron and piled a round tray high with all the customary specialties of the season except the oranges and Ise prawns, which he left out in order to remind his family of those times of hardship to which every small merchant is susceptible. In the same spirit his mother made a humble broth of rice cakes boiled with sweet potatoes and radishes. Since it was believed to be especially lucky if one "forgot" to include the rice cakes, the family now made sure that all was in accord with the prescribed custom.

On every New Year's Day the father would also take out his will and rewrite the document as his ceremonial First Writing of the New Year. Then he would return it to its case, apply his seal, and tuck the will away under the family's Buddhist altar until the following year. When he had first started this custom, his cash fortune was some five hundred and seventy *kamme*. Every year thereafter he wrote down the new totals, and after forty-one years of following this ritual he finally passed away at the age of eighty-three. The entire family gathered together on the forty-ninth day after his death, and when they examined

He dreamily stretched out alongside Yoshino on the futon bedding. . . . Just as he was settling down to the evening's business, however, the front door of the house suddenly burst open. Through the thin walls he could hear a runner delivering a message to one of the guests in the next room. "Sir, a letter has come from your home."

his will they discovered that, aside from jewelry and other valuables, a family fortune of four thousand seven hundred and nineteen *kamme* was stored in three sections of the cellar vault. The father's last testament read as follows:

> Since this enormous amount of money is due to the shrewd investments my eldest son made in one year by cornering the rice and oil markets, I bequeath my entire estate to him and direct his younger brothers to comport themselves according to his instructions.
>
> Especially in the case of my youngest son, we find here a man not much accustomed to the merchant's life of checking weights on a balance and examining account books. The explanation of this is simple—he has never been one to devote his life to the pursuit of beauty or the satisfaction of his appetites, or to go about humming the latest tunes. He would neither rush off to the hairdresser's when some new style appeared, nor take those late-night strolls, with all that they so often entail. Instead, he has kept his mind on the transience of life. They say that in this fleeting world if a man has failed to demonstrate any sense of virtue, then he might as well not have lived at all. When one looks at the figure of an average man, he may appear to be a fool, but there are also elements of wisdom in his being. So my instructions to you, my son, are to search out some Pure Land temple where the abbot has both a pretty daughter and a large number of parishioners, and have yourself adopted for three hundred *kamme*.*

---

* In the Pure Land Shinshu sect, the abbotship was hereditary, hence the advantages of marrying into his family. Under such circumstances, the young man was expected to provide his own "dowry."

And now for my second son. Even to your own parents, you are simply unfathomable. For the most part you have an inventive and clever nature, and we've never known you to take second place in anything to anyone. You received training in the traditional musical instruments, following the teachings first established by the great Noh masters Kanze, Komparu, Hosho, and Kongo, and passed down through the generations by the strictest lines of direct, personal transmission; you resided at Shinzaike ward in Kyoto, where famous linked-verse masters took you under their wings; your *haikai* verses were so good that Nishiyama Soin visited our home; you were instructed in the Ikenobo school's esoteric style of flower arrangement; you demonstrated your talents so well in *kemari** football that you were allowed to wear the prestigious purple trousers; in the tea ceremony you learned the Kanamori transmission of the Sowa school; you heard Utsunomiya Ton'an lecture on the Confucian Way; your skill in *go* is so great that even *go* masters are careful in the handicap they allow you; in archery you were trained in the style of Itchu until you could claim top-rank marksmanship; Yamaguchi Enkyu taught you the subtleties of the ten incenses and their combinations; and you followed the instructions of an expert in court etiquette and became quite proficient in it yourself. As if this were not enough, you learned to play the *biwa* and *koto* from the great master Hayama; Iwai and Gendayu taught you to sing; Yashichi taught you improvisation; Omu (the Parrot) Kichihyoe taught

---

* A game popular among the aristocracy. The players formed a circle, and the object was to keep the ball in the air by using one's feet.

you mimicry; and you can carry a tune as well as any professional.

When a person excels in everything he touches, word of his talents spreads far and wide and everyone extols him to the skies, but he never comes to learn anything about how one actually makes a living in this world. The more bold a disposition one receives at birth, the less likely he is to really consider the demands of the moment. If you put money in his hands, swindlers and crooks will descend from all sides. No matter how much money he had to start with, between his investments in new rice land, development of mines, and sponsorship of the theater on one hand, and his playing the banker at some gaming table on the other, he will lose it all down to the very last penny.

My son, by the time you were only seven years old, you had already stolen one *ryo* worth of coins with which you bought a kite string. And when you were nine, you had twenty-three *bu* in a pouch slung from your belt. Ever since your childhood you have stolen money, and, what with your brazen disposition, I hardly think you will be of much use in the world of business.

When you lived in the Capital, and later in Osaka, you built a splendid little villa for yourself. You had your sweetheart and another girl to look after all your errands, and if you count up all the other servants that were at your disposal, there must have been altogether seven people to support, eight with you included. To cover your personal expenses and the expenses of your household I had to contribute ten *ryo* toward your allowance at the end of each month, and I feel no obligation to hand you a single copper more to endorse this extravagance. Once I'm gone, you certainly will not be one to observe the fasts on the anniversary of my death.

During this past confinement of mine you made your fleeting attendances at my bedside only to keep up appearances, and even then all you did was just stand there and yawn. In the very next room you would make every kind of sporting conversation, and on four or five occasions I heard you say things like: "Oh yes, now that father has lived to such a ripe old age, it is about time that he made his final journey to that better land. There really isn't a single advantage to living such an awfully long life. Your eyes grow so dim that you lose all sense of how the flowers are blooming, and your ears get so feeble that the sound of the cuckoo is nothing more than a memory. Your teeth get to wobbling so much in your mouth that fish loses its flavor, and your legs are so weak that you need a cane just to hobble into the parlor. He's become the most dreadful bore to his daughter-in-law, and each day he clings on is just another day wasted. Before we spend any more money on medicines, I would rather see him out of his misery."

There isn't a grain of good in a person like that, but it is my fate as a parent that I must still look upon even this child with pity and compassion; I have therefore included various provisions in my will to guide and inform your future actions.

From that day on, the second son was filled with shame by the sincere concern of his father. Actually, this kind of son might just as well not have been born at all, but in our times there is no dearth of similarly minded offspring. Is this not just one more instance of each of us getting his due? If the parents are wealthy, then unfilial behavior is not nearly so noticeable, but if the parents are poor, then it is hard to cover up even the slightest act of wickedness. The degree of wealth or poverty of the parents is what spells the difference between the advantages to be enjoyed by the children. To be born into a wealthy and prominent household is one's just harvest for virtuous deeds performed in a previous incarnation. In any case, be sure to do good to your fellow man and keep your livelihood in the forefront of your mind.

The sakè sold by the Ikeda and Itami families in the village of Wayside starts with only the finest water; the rice is then carefully selected and no expense is spared for the yeast. Women are not allowed in the sakè storehouses during their courses, and workers change their sandals each time they enter or leave the brewing areas. Thus, by paying careful attention to every last detail, the great sakè houses prosper one beside the other. Sakè distributors like the Masuya, Maruya, Aburaya, Yamamotoya, Suya, Obeya, Yamatoya, Manganjiya, Kamoya, Shimizuya, and still others have all made their fortunes. Under the divine auspices of Matsuno'o, the God of Sakè, their finest brews have been protected and preserved for us. Now that the leaves and branches of a thousand cryptomeria rest perfectly still, this village called Wayside in Settsu Province is no longer quite so obscure.

• 2 • Secrets of turning mushrooms into money

With the sun by day and the moon by night to shine upon the truth, the people of our divine country have always trodden the straight and narrow path, showing their reverence for the principles of honesty and straightforwardness. Our people observe the courtesies due their superiors and behave with compassion to those below themselves. Those who provide for themselves are said to be their own masters, but those who live the life of a merchant, whether in the Capital or in the countryside, must take care to never run afoul of the law or the customs.

In ancient times, the wise were rewarded with lofty positions and titles, and the simple-minded were recognized as such. Although people back then were categorized according to intelligence, nowadays virtually everyone seems to be born with a sufficient amount of sense and reason, and each gives the impression of knowing this and that without necessarily having had any training. There isn't a soul left whom you can trust to be a fool at first glance. We now live in an age when people are no longer deceived by the run-of-the-mill trickery of corrupt Buddhist priests or *yin-yang* diviners and their ilk. If they were simply to tell the truth! If even the magician were to show his audience the secrets of his tricks! If the street corner evangelist were actually to speak a few words of the Buddha and admit that it hurts when one does not have enough to eat, then even he would be called an honest priest and showered with contributions.

As proof of the fact that we live in an age when people uphold the laws, an age in which lies have no place, let me point to the cases involving sales on credit, or to short-term loans where even if the customer claims that he never received his goods or money and there is no receipt to prove the contrary, the account is settled, despite some troublesome litigation, exclusively on the strength of the lender's word as to his recollection of the account book.

Now, some time ago, in a warehouse by the dockyards, there operated a wholesaler who was a cut above others in his contempt for parting with money. One New Year's Eve, when all was in a state of hustle and bustle, he handed over the sum of thirteen and one-third *ryo* to an agent of one of his suppliers. The agent correctly noted the name and amount in his account book and applied the proper seal but absentmindedly departed without putting the money into his purse. Afterward, the wholesaler hid the money among his own belongings. The next day, when the agent called again, the wholesaler insisted, "What do you mean? I've already paid you!" The agent shed a virtual fountain of tears over the dire straits in which he now found himself, but even though he swore the most solemn oaths by all the gods and Buddhas that he was telling the truth, and even though he begged forgiveness for his carelessness, his pleas fell on deaf ears. With nowhere left to turn, the agent removed himself to the Pure Land temple at which he normally worshiped and there committed suicide as a final gesture to his employer for his loss.

Of course, after his suicide there was no longer any doubt as to whether he had absconded with the cash. Criticism of the wholesaler's harshness poured in from all sides, and eventually his business declined. Then his wife, who up to this time had produced any number of children with no snarls in the deliveries, gave birth to a child without any arms as a retribution for the evil of her husband. This is the same child who last year, when the carnival came to Dotombori, was on display under the name Bottle-Child Mantaro. The shame of this family was exposed to all the world in this way, and, in the end, both the family and its business vanished from sight. Unbridled greed, no doubt, will exact its own revenge.

Now, as we all know, "What will be, will be," and there are many, many ways for us to get by in the world. However, if we are talking about a businessman without capital of his own, then no matter what talents or wit he may have at his disposal, sooner or later the interest rates on his loans will drive him into the ground, and he will end up working for someone else. A person with a solid financier to back him automatically has a certain freedom of movement, and whenever he sets his mind to it he can engage in speculation or cornering the market, often showing profit for his efforts. If we were to examine the biography of the courtier Tung Fang-shuo in the *History of the Former Han,* we would learn that in a year when the roots of the maize plant point toward the south and the rest of the plant grows tall, winds stiff enough to blow over a millstone will come just before the harvest. But while we might know that such-and-such is a good year for buying grains and cereals, we would still lack the money. It certainly is a hectic world in which we live.

The sixty days that lie between each of the five major festivals pass by as quickly as a dream. No sooner have the sprays of mountain shrubs with which we decorated our sea-bream offerings of the New Year begun to wither than we begin to hear the voice of the sagebrush hawker peddling his wares in preparation for the Festival of the Third Month. Even now we can still see stuck here and there among the eaves of houses those irises left over from the Festival of the Fifth Month, and it is already time to hang out the lanterns for the Festival of All Souls. All this excitement is enough to make our hearts leap, and if we pause to remember that it is on the eve of each of the holidays that our bills fall due for payment, it is really enough to make our hearts skip a beat. It is funny the way our heads spin so unexpectedly upon seeing the bill from the liquor store for holiday chrysanthemum sakè after the Festival of the Ninth Month when our rice balls wrapped in lotus petals for the Festival of All Souls have not even had a chance to grow cold.

Just recently someone obliged to me gave me a generous holiday gift of a string of dried cuttlefish and twenty dried barracuda on a lovely lacquered stand. But since the customary gift of this season is chestnuts, which happen to be unusually expensive this year, it seems that the moving spirit behind this gift was more mercenary than charitable.

Just when you stop and think that you can allow yourself a bit of a breather from paying all those holiday bills in the hundred or so days between the Festival of the Ninth Month and New Year's Day, you realize that what makes the New Year's celebration different from other holidays is that you have to settle every last one of your outstanding debts.

Hayashi Kan'emon was a merchant for whom business

had gone just as he had foreseen, and yet he still found himself short of year-end funds. He turned to his wife when she was in an especially good mood and tried out his little plan on her.

"You know the Pure Land Monto Temple which we've been so close to over the years? Since it's been doing so well for itself lately, I think I might stroll over and say, 'The year is rapidly drawing to a close, and I would be ever so grateful if I might borrow eight *ryo* to tide over my accounts.' "

His wife just looked at him a bit skeptically while holding a sakè cup in one hand, and casually replied, "Well, I don't know. Wouldn't five *ryo* be perfectly sufficient? We can get by with that, and since the anniversary of Lord Shinran's death is coming up at the end of the eleventh month, it might help us with our contribution."

But her husband was not to be put off so easily. Despite all reason he resolutely proclaimed, "With the abbot's help, we're going to make it through the holidays!"

And so every day from then on he spared no words in flattering the abbot and treating him to tea and tobacco. Every five days Hayashi brought some special gift, presenting it on his hands and knees. When the first mushrooms of the season appeared, he prepared a package of them, even though they were outrageously expensive, and gave them to the abbot while claiming they were a present from his relatives in Saga. In the tenth month, before the first frost, Hayashi showed the abbot a wild dove prepared to look like a souvenir gift. This he gave to him, saying "Just a little something from my family in the mountains." He gave pork rice-balls to the temple as an offering for the success of his progeny, and he even remembered the abbot's mother—she got a pillbox hat! Eventually, Hayashi resorted to any conceivable excuse for visiting the temple, such as informing the abbot that when changing the guard during his nightly shift on the neighborhood patrol he had seen a cat fall from a ledge and injure itself. When the parish wives had their rice-ball bazaar, Hayashi accompanied his wife and, while she attended to the fire, he drew water for the special rice tub, working away with what for him was unprecedented vigor.

Finally, on the twentieth day of the twelfth month, Hayashi made his earnest request to the abbot, asking him for five hundred *me** to cover accounts. The abbot gave his consent. Then, on New Year's Eve at ten P.M., Hayashi signed a contract to pay back the entire sum at a monthly interest of one and a half *bu*. Among the terms was his promise that " . . . if for any reason I am found delinquent in the repayment of this loan, my only daughter will be sold to a licensed house of prostitution, with the proceeds from said sale reverting to the monastery."

As he left the temple he thanked everyone down to the lowliest employee, saying things like, "It would be difficult indeed for me to forget the tremendous kindness which you have shown me today." This was rather pointless, since none of them had even heard of the matter.

The year quickly drew to a close, and on the fourth day of the first month when he was taking stock, Hayashi neglected to include his miscellaneous expenses into his account book, thinking that five hundred *me* was really a rather paltry sum to have borrowed. He then wasted eighty-four *momme* six *bu* and five *rin* buying something or other. This kind of expenditure is truly what makes the life of a poor person so difficult as he tries to scrape by in the world.

From that year on, whenever Hayashi and his wife would

---

*There were sixty *me* per *ryo*.

confer in private they both agreed the only thing that makes money in this world is more money and that working your fingers to the bone only helps someone else. Ignoring any thought of keeping up appearances, they decided that only the future held any promise for happiness. They left Osaka after selling off their stock of fashionable Nara sandals for only three *mon* a pair and hid themselves away in the small town of Oriono just south of Sumiyoshi, where Hayashi's wife had been raised. By night Hayashi sold lantern oil, and during the day he took advantage of his ability to write a character or two by taking responsibility for instructing the village children in calligraphy. In his classes, he "clipped the wild grasses" of these undisciplined children, and, starting with the basics, he taught the youngsters how to read.

Since he had no knowledge of those Noh-drama texts with which school children were trained, he found himself in a bit of a fix, which he remedied by journeying each day to Osaka where an old friend of his gave him lessons that he in turn would pass on to his country pupils. Although he had learned the Kanehira style of Noh chanting, from time to time his students might ask to hear the Ohara Goko or Gendayu styles or one of the so-called Outer One Hundred plays of the Noh repertory. Whenever this happened, he would promise to deliver the lesson on the following day—teachers having always found it difficult to admit to not knowing something. Relying on the help of his cohort in Osaka he could continue to claim to his students that "Whatever you might like to know, just ask, and I will produce it," even though the answer might be one more day in the coming. Because of these boasts, the village headman would occasionally call on Hayashi if there was an obscure character that he was unable to locate in the *Setsuyoshu* dictionary. But

The only thing that makes money in this world is more money and . . . working your fingers to the bone only helps someone else. . . . By night Hayashi sold lantern oil, and during the day he took advantage of his ability to write a character or two by taking responsibility for instructing the village children in calligraphy. In his classes, he "clipped the

SOME FINAL WORDS OF ADVICE · 52

wild grasses" of these undisciplined children, and, starting with the basics, he taught the youngsters how to read. Since he had no knowledge of those Noh-drama texts with which school children were trained, he found himself in a bit of a fix.

not once was Hayashi able to produce a satisfactory answer, so the situation was not really all that good.

At first the families of his students showered him with presents during the wheat and cotton harvests and at the time for making ritual offerings of the first-picked grains. Hayashi thought to himself that teaching was actually more profitable than any of his businesses had been, but one by one his students began to withdraw from the little school. Once again, then, Hayashi found himself in trouble. Day and night he devised new schemes for making his fortune, but still he could not come up with even thirty coppers at the end of any one day.

One morning Hayashi noticed that the fire he had lit to heat the kettle the night before was still burning. Thinking this odd, he examined what had been used for fuel and noticed that the combination of knotgrass and twigs from the mad-apple tree produced embers that would not die out. Realizing that this was a gem of information unknown to anyone else, he went down to Edo without a penny to his name and there collaborated with a metal smith. It was in this way that the pocket heater was invented.

From that snowy twelfth month on, he marketed his device. Elderly and retired people found it especially comforting, and samurai warriors made use of it during their turns on night watch. As it grew in popularity, Hayashi hung out his shingle that called the invention "The Perpetual Flame —Good for Hibachi Braziers and Pocket Lighters." His invention sold well, and before long he became quite wealthy. With his new-found fortune, he opened up a bank in the Ginza section of Edo. No one knew just how many thousands of *ryo* he had tucked away in its vaults, but in his own quiet way Hayashi Kan'emon found himself the head of a discreet but prosperous enterprise.

If one were to compare Hayashi's bank with the very reputable Mitani Bank in Suruga-cho or with any of the other banks which boast of having small mountains of gold in their vaults, one would have to say Hayashi's bank was second to none. He attended to the needs of powerful daimyo no matter how great their requirements, and as the family's prosperity continued, he sequestered his wife and daughter in an out-of-the-way place where they could not be seen by members of the lower classes. On some days he would take the family out in his palanquin to see the cherry blossoms in Ueno; on other days they would all go boating on the Sumida River. In every way they enjoyed the pleasures of an elegant life " . . . with cherry and plum blossoms" as a backdrop.

Even after they attained the graceful presence of people who one would assume had been raised in the Capital, and were enjoying a lifetime full of wonders, they never forgot that it was all thanks to Heaven's smiling upon them when times were so rough that Hayashi's wife had to help eke out the family's living. They were always grateful for the blessing of being able to enjoy a peaceful life. They made their fortune quite literally out of ashes, and the continued prosperity of their household was as certain as the never-ending chain of smoke billowing out of Mount Fuji.

◆ 3 ◆ From old account books to eighteen employees

Just as there is nothing quite as useful as wealth and fame for covering up one's wrongdoings, there is nothing like poverty for insuring that all of one's shameful acts will come before the public eye. A prosperous person can utter any number of perversities, and yet people will let them pass. But if some pauper scarcely able to scrape by should say something, no one will give him an ear, even if what the pauper says to him is for his own benefit. It hardly needs repeating that, no matter what the circumstances may be, unless you have money your life in this world will be of no consequence. While all of this is something any merchant should know, many still forget that their livelihoods should be their paramount concern. They are continually having their wares stolen from under their noses on moonlit nights, and it is in the midst of some pointless conversation with the bill collector that they suddenly realize just how harsh the air can be under the new moon of New Year's night.

Nowadays, one can often hear people claim there is no

business to be had. This is quite different from what the figures tell us, for a comparison of present conditions with those of former times will show that there is appreciably more commerce going on. To cite just one example, on Sakai Street in Osaka there is a lacquerware shop that sells bowls, trays, nested boxes, and a thousand and one other things. If we were to examine the shop's old account books from our parent's generation in the 1630s, we would find that the total sales for any one year were less than seven *kamme*. These scant earnings supported a total of six people, including the shop owner, and left the owner enough to provide New Year's presents of clothing to all his employees and to prepare the customary rice cakes like everyone else.

All accounts due for receipt or payment were settled between the twenty-fifth and twenty-eighth days of the twelfth month, and on New Year's Eve the owner would gather around him all his old friends who were no longer quite so active and hold a grand party at which the cares and woes of the past year could be laid to rest. His friends would dine on duck soup with grilled yellowtail and laugh heartily together over cups of sakè. As far as they were concerned there was not a care in the world worth worrying about, for their affairs were in order.

But now, in our own day and age, there is ever so much more business transacted at this same shop than in the time of the present owner's father. Each year the sales register shows transactions of over forty *kamme,* and even the number of employees has increased to eighteen. Thus, for one to say that somehow there is less business than in olden times is surely not borne out by the facts. And yet, it really is harder than ever to make it through the year.

The owner now goes to his bank and takes out one-day loans or two-day silver promissory notes. Ignoring the fact that interest rates are as high as twenty percent, he goes ahead and borrows anyway. When it comes time to pay up, he hands over whatever is sufficient to put off the creditors till another day, busily tapping away at his scales right up until the first guests come to pay their New Year's respects. Then, when he knows that he has finally paid off all the creditors, he happily dozes off, using his leather purse for a pillow. All that is left in the purse is some eighteen *momme,* which are probably counterfeit anyway. With nothing left in his cashbox and inkstone case, he leaves them unlocked, not even bothering to sweep up the flakes from the cords which at one time held strings of coppers. The ashes from the bill collector's smoking are still all in a heap on the tray, but he pays them no mind and snores peacefully through the night, without stirring until dawn, by which time the wick on his night lamp has burned down to its cup.

On New Year's morning his mother is the first to rise from her bed, and she immediately awakens the scullery maid, who haughtily puffs up her cheeks in a most disagreeable manner upon receiving orders to heat up a pot with some bean stalks and set the table. When the mother orders Kyushichi, one of the houseboys, to draw the ritual First Water of the New Year, he answers her: "Get one of those who have been working here longer! I can't be expected to know how you like it done! But as long as you're heating up some rice balls, I'll gladly eat to my health!"

The head clerk of the family shop, putting off his morning duties, rolls over in bed to lounge against Kyushichi.*

---

* As unmarried male employees of the household, it was not unusual for the clerk and the houseboy to share the same quarters. Their bedding, while separate, would have been layed out on the floor in such a manner

"Don't try to wake me till I'm good and ready," he grumbles. "Did you know that the young man who works across the street has been employed there three years less than I've been employed here, and this year his employer is already giving him fancy clothes cut from Hino silk and even short swords like the samurai wear? And what do I get? Just a checkered cotton jacket that I'd be embarrassed to be seen in outside the gate."

And even from the lowly busboys: "Looks as though the god Ebisu isn't smiling on us this year—no salted sea bream with our New Year's soup!" Pouting over such trivial things as receiving a cotton sash instead of a silk one or getting leather-thonged sandals instead of ones with leather soles and linings, the other servants ignore their orders, acting as if someone else should have been asked. If there is a lesson to be learned from all this, it is that there is no sense in having a house full of servants.

On one of these particularly trying New Year's mornings, the shop owner's mother awoke to the realization that all the discord in the household was due to her son's failure to carry out his responsibilities as head of the family. She burst into tears, and as she called forth memories of her late husband, she placed some incense and fresh flowers at the household Buddhist altar and wailed, "All that one gets from a long life is disappointment!"

Her shrieks awoke the entire household with a start. What saddened the woman was not so much her own unfortunate circumstances but rather the fact that her son's status in the community was being jeopardized by his extraordinarily

---

that the clerk would literally need to do no more than roll over in order to lounge against Kyushichi. They can be seen, still lying in bed, in the upper left of the illustration on page 61.

unfilial behavior. After all, it was only natural that her female disposition should find the rumors and gossip so humiliating.

"How can it be," lamented her son, "that a shop of such long standing can find itself time and again so hard-pressed to pay its bills when business now seems better than ever?"

Taking the opportunity to say what had been on her mind for some time, his mother drew up her knees and, just like a man, pounded the *tatami* mat with her fist. "Let me tell you what things were like here when your father was alive. By the time the sparrows began to chirp, I would already have blackened my teeth and arranged my hair. While the scullery maid drew water from the well, I lit the fire under the kettle, and in the time it took her to fix the rice, I put away the bedding and the linen. I had the houseboy clean the lanterns and then polish the smoking pipes with the same oil-soaked rag. After that, I had him wipe the grooves of the sliding doors, and just so that nothing would go to waste, anything to be thrown out was put into a bin for the dustman. In this way no nook or cranny escaped attention.

"Whenever a servant was dispatched to the theater, he was sent out before breakfast so that his hunger would hurry him home, and if a servant was needed for an errand near the licensed quarters, we gave him his duties without advance notice and sent him from the storeroom before he had time to change his sash or fetch his purse. We all cooked simple Kaga rice in the same pot and ate the same humble fare of plain broth and sardines set before us on the table. Since there was no distinction between family and staff, no one complained when we didn't prepare special dishes like fish salad on the first and last days of the month. Even on ritual fast days with just a morning and evening dish of

On one of these particularly trying New Year's mornings, the shop owner's mother awoke to the realization that all the discord in the household was due to her son's failure to carry out his responsibilities as head of the family. She burst into tears . . . and wailed, "All that one gets from a long life is disappointment!"

pickles, we would all say, 'we have this thanks to our master,' while picking up our chopstick boxes. On chilly days, the servants would say, 'It is because of our new padded clothing that we don't feel the blustery cold.' Since even small details like dirty collars were never tolerated, things did not get out of hand.

"I always appeared in a pale blue cotton kimono with a pongee sash. When invited to a wedding reception, I wore a silk kimono with a pattern of chrysanthemums scattered on a pale blue background, a figured satin sash, and purple leather split-toe slippers.

"You might think that we were a bit extravagant, but let's look at what your bride wears. She can usually be found in padded, white silk formal underwear. Over that she has a floral-patterned kimono, and on top of that, a black silk outer kimono with matching lining and a round crest of wisteria blossoms so large that it looks as if someone hammered it out. The cuffs of her sleeves are as wide as an actor's, and that patterned satin sash of hers is so wide that you can't even tell where her hips begin. For two *chokin* she had a pocket comb made to order from translucent bits of the finest tortoise shell, and she had her silver styling comb decorated with gold-plated crests. She wears a coral comb in the front of her hair and has a special wire braid to keep the hair from her neck.

"Even though her face is pale enough without any makeup, she dissolves a royal white powder, worn only by ladies of the Imperial Palace, in water from melted snow and ice, and then she smears this mixture on her face as many as two hundred times. She lavishes her hands and feet in lemon bath oils; she drapes a purple quilt over the *kotatsu* footwarmer and has a light brown satin afghan; she wraps her toothbrush in a paper hankie; she burns fine aloe incense in tobacco embers; she takes her green tea in a deep cup; and with a copy of *The Tale of Genji* always close at hand, she spends her years at work daydreaming about fanciful love affairs. She takes her carriage out to view the cherry blossoms in the spring and to see the changing colors in the fall, and whenever a new play appears, she takes the best seats in the house. Wherever she goes, she is accompanied by her housemaid, parlormaid, and seamstress. I can tell you that even if we saved pins in the storehouse, there still would not be enough to support this extravagance. Wasteful expenditure within the household is one certain way to ruin a fortune.

"While your lady, to whom you have pledged your troth, fashions herself like some strumpet for only you to see, you hide from her the bitter reality. If one takes a fancy to go to some elegant place downtown, it's perfectly natural to wear one's best clothes, since that's the way people dress there. But to parade around the house all day in the finest lingerie with a red gauze undersash is a useless extravagance. Even if you wear ordinary clothes, they still welcome you to the licensed quarters if you have enough money, and nowadays, this is all it takes to be reckoned a wise man."

Now, on the subject of brides, regardless of whether her groom immediately assumes the responsibilities as household head, one can expect the two of them to put up with one another for only about a year. The new wife, for her part, curries the favor of her husband, and fearing the demands on her which abdication of family leadership would entail, she is careful to behave in an agreeable manner toward both the male and female servants. Moreover, since in her mind divorce would be a crisis of the highest magnitude, she wholeheartedly prays for the future prosperity of her household.

But in the meantime a son is born, and as one might expect of a family with ample resources, the child's upbringing is entrusted to a nurse. Nonetheless, the wife's figure begins to deteriorate, and suddenly she looks much older and more haggard than she really is. When her husband recalls how lovely she once was, his romantic impulses begin to stray, and this makes her all the more jealous.

Not even twenty years old, the wife's speech becomes terribly coarse, and she might easily be found saying the following words to the maid who accompanied her from her parents' village: "Just look at how bad off I am! I had offers of marriage from the owner of a draper's shop in Fushimi, and the proprietor of a liquor store in Temma was also after my hand. And of all the offers placed before me, I had to be fooled by this lacquerware man. As I later learned, the one who really tricked me was the go-between, that fellow Kyusai from the Hirano store—the one that I know from my Buddhist chanting circle.

"Why, I've been so worn out by my miseries that I know I'm not long for this world. You know that silk jacket I had with the embroidered golden phoenix? I made it into an altar cover and gave it to the temple. And that kimono with the embroidered flower-cart pattern? Well, now it's a drape for one of the statues. I've had my personal things burned, because when you haven't a speck of dust or an ash left in this Floating World, then there's nothing to give you any trouble. But since my only child hasn't had smallpox yet, who knows what will become of him?"

From then on, she does not even prepare a meal that would keep the mice happy, nor can she be bothered to press her husband's trousers. When he is away on business, she prepares all her own favorite dishes for supper, and then when he is about to return she says, "Oh, I suppose it's time for the old fool to be on his way home." She lowers the wicks on the oil lamps and takes the peel from the persimmon on which she has been munching and throws it where it won't be noticed.

She suddenly complains about strange creaks and groans in a room that in fact is perfectly sound, and she loves making a nuisance of herself and gloats as the family falls into decline. The way a woman's heart can change and change again over time is frightening indeed.

As for the husband, he is nagged from the moment he awakens till it reaches the point where everything his wife does seems offensive. In the end his only recourse is to draw up papers for a divorce.

There is nothing in this world quite as injurious to a man's position in life as a divorce. For the woman, too, even should she choose to remarry, her second marriage will never be as good as her first. In any case, it is a good thing for a man to choose a wife of a class lower than his own, disregarding whatever society might have to say about the affair. For her part, a bride might also find it agreeable when someone from a lowlier background asks for her hand. But, just as the saying "you can't hang a bell from a lantern" implies, it is only a matter of time before the flames of an ill-suited marriage are forever extinguished. In our example of the family in the shop, we have seen how trying to better the ways of one's in-laws can bring on the downfall of an entire household.

◆ 4 ◆ Omi province, mosquito nets, a clever woman

Surely there is nothing quite as annoying as when wives fuss over whether their kitchen utensils are better than those of their neighbors, and this practice often leads to a significant drain on our country's resources.

In the Nakachoja ward in the northern part of the Capital, there was a tailor shop where apprentices and hired help worked patiently and carefully sewing mosquito nets of silk gauze. Now while there were many other things one could see in the Capital, the number of people crowding to look at this shop's wares grew so great that one could barely press through the mob. The peasant women selling homemade charcoal were a comical sight as they struggled in vain to wend their way through the crowded street, but even their odd appearance—they were dressed in stiffly starched skirts of double thickness—could not compete with the wonder of the mosquito nets in drawing a crowd.

At each corner of these nets was sewn a red piece of cloth woven in the Szechuan style and cut into the shape of a chrysanthemum blossom, as well as deep crimson tassels to which were attached incense pouches. There were decorations of coral and lapis lazuli, silver hanging hooks, and gold rings. Sewn at regular intervals between the seams were tinkling bells, and from each of the loops hung a five-colored tassel. Along the borders were embroidered views of a pair of frolicking mandarin ducks, and beside the river banks where these ducks sported were scenes of willow trees, their branches piled high with snow.

Since one had only to look at this wintry river scene to feel its coolness, one could easily envy the lucky fellow who could forget the summer heat while sleeping under such a net. Anyone who saw these nets might easily say to himself, "Since this shop is close to the Imperial Palace, I suppose some prominent family has had such a net made for its delight. Could even the Buddha's bedchamber, which they say is in Paradise, have fittings such as these? It's truly a wonder!"

The owner of the shop stepped into the middle of the crowd, lay down on the ground, and, propping his head on his arm, said, "Please excuse me, everyone. Imagine for a moment, a dream scene. In it a young man joins his bride under one of these splendid mosquito nets with a Floating World double mattress and an oversized pillow for two. It is the fruits of good deeds done in a former existence that account for his good fortune, and he now plants the first seeds of his love.

"Now, your average soul couldn't possibly afford this kind of bridal net, though it is certainly a reasonable purchase for a merchant, and of course, for a nobleman or a daimyo. A net like this costs two *kan* six hundred *me*. No matter how rich you may be, you need one of these to prove it.

"But after all, since the only purpose of these nets is to protect you from mosquito bites, you can just sew some red loops and borders on a piece of Omi cotton netting and there will be no way for a mosquito to force himself through." By the time he finished his story, the crowd had pressed so close around him that he felt as cramped as if he really were lying under a three-by-six-foot net.

The Omi mosquito-net business had its beginnings in the town of Yawata and spread from there throughout the country. Among the various people making their living from these nets was a certain man named Ogiya. Formerly, Ogiya had operated a small liquor store that sold rice on the side. His wife was a clever woman who always carried a measuring box about with her. If a poor person wished to buy some small amount of, say, not more than half a gallon of rice or sakè, she never thought of the profit and always gave full measure, thus giving the impression that business was good. Since, before long, word of her honesty spread throughout Omi Province, when people from villages and hamlets, even those deep in the mountains, came to the city's market to shop, they would stop at the store, press their way through the crowds at its doors, and order all sorts of things before returning home. Thus at the end of each day the shopowner and his wife would have a "mountain" of copper coins and a "valley" of silver ones. They rapidly became quite wealthy and as time went on, the reputation of this shop grew to the point where people used its finest Morohaku sakè for sore throats and coughs instead of medicine!

When a family becomes wealthy, life acquires a blissful effortlessness not unlike what a sailor experiences when the wind is blowing stiff and cool from behind. The Ogiya household was no exception. In due course, the family took mosquito netting from Takamiya in Omi Province and marketed it in branch stores throughout the provinces. One in particular, the Higashi-no-Toin shop on Fourth Avenue in the Capital, sold each year as much cloth as could be carried by a thousand packhorses. Another branch store, this one in Osaka, did as well in *tatami* matting, and eventually Ogiya became one of the country's great financial magnates. While it is impossible to say just how many of these mosquito nets were produced in the following years, one might well imagine that sales reached the distant corners of the world.

Every day, the more than eighty weavers and some fifty seamstresses who worked on the loops and borders of the nets came to the shop, and the scene when they were all lined up in the canteen looked like one from some fabled Isle of Women. However, among all these workers, there was not one who carried herself with the grace of a lady from the Capital. Tama had a scar, Suji had all-too-prominent hips, Take's mouth was too wide, and so on. At mealtimes a large tub, filled with rice and attached to a wagon, was drawn around the canteen by three houseboys, and the sight of the girls all in neat rows, each poised for her turn to ladle rice from the tub, suggested the many legs of a centipede. Only the god Bishamonten from Kurama Temple could protect a kitchen of this size, and since the shop was in operation throughout the year, it required considerable ingenuity to manage so many people.

Twice a year, at the Festival of All Souls and at New Year's, the owner of the shop ordered presents of clothing for all his employees after consulting with them about their favorite colors and special requests for seals or crests. Moreover, since there were also many supervisors, preparations for the New Year's presents were usually under way by the eighth month. Every last detail was always attended to.

Even though this shop was an enterprise of such magnitude, at its heart it was still just a family with a master and three or four dependents. Nonetheless, it was an act of incomparable generosity on the master's part that by his individual efforts hundreds of workers should find employment. And it was a consequence of the benevolence of his heart that these workers obeyed him like so many trees and grasses bending before the wind. For years and years the Ogiya household had in its garden an old, gracefully shaped pine tree that was no less imposing than any of the thousand stately pines of Kitano or the ten thousand pines of Awaji. It was a pine whose view would be enjoyed for a thousand years.

Well, be that as it may, there is nothing in this world as varied as the ways in which people make their livings. Even in the backwoods of Omi Province there are men like Ogiya. One man who eventually found himself in the out-of-the-way place of Hachiman village in Omi was Yorozuya Jimbei. He was born and raised in the Capital on Kyogoku Avenue, a street known for its temples, so even before he was born his stomach knew well the sweet waters of that city.

He learned many of the wise old tricks that Kyoto people know so well, but even though anyone with a decent living should be able to support a family of three to five people, it was a source of considerable embarrassment to him that he could not, in the end, even scrape up enough to feed himself and his wife. He was so talented in calligraphy that he could easily have worked as a professional sign-and-billboard painter, his powers of calculation were so good that even difficult division was not beyond him, and from time to time representatives from banks came to ask his expert opinion on whether their silver was genuine or counterfeit. He was able to give singularly fine counsel on virtually every matter, and there was nothing he could not handle. He was a gifted raconteur, and even knew his way around a kitchen. He was as good as anyone at chanting in the Noh style, and had yet to meet his match in *go* or chess. And when he wasn't occupied with his own affairs, he was never too busy to lend someone else a hand.

But he was always short of money, and business would just not go his way in the Capital. He stocked items geared to a seasonal trade, such as ribald books in the spring, folding fans in the summer, festival accessories for the autumn, and overcoats in the winter. Every year for some twenty years he would pack up his wares and set out for Omi Province to make sales, but in the course of one year he would not be home to see his wife's face for more than twenty days. Since he had learned popular anecdotes and songs in the Capital, he used them day and night to entertain and to curry the good will of his clients, with the result that his marriage became little more than a dining arrangement. For many years he had managed to keep his savings at a level of two hundred *me,* never more or less. Then an aunt on his mother's side who lived alone on Shujaku Avenue passed away, alas, quite suddenly. Since except for himself there was no one to mourn her and to see to her burial, the entire expense of thirty *me* fell to him. Though he tried every possible means of economizing for the following four or five years, he was unable to resave those thirty *me*, and he wished there were some way he could return his savings to their former level of two hundred.

He made inquiries to the keeper of a hostel and got a job procuring children to be taken from the Capital out to the country for the purpose of adoption by families short of hands. For this he was awarded an unexpectedly large commission of sixty silver *me*. "This has been the stroke of a

Although he could have hired a horse to take him as far as Otsu, he chose instead to walk—just to be on the safe side. The twilight bell of the Ishiyama Temple was just tolling as he was passing through the Awazu moor when two men who looked to be masterless samurai jumped out of a grove of pines and said, "We know you're going to find this heartless, but it's a

difficult time of year for all of us, and just give a thought to how desperate we must be. All we ask for is what we need for the New Year." . . . *Since his pleas for mercy fell on deaf ears, Jimbei did what he had to and handed over the silver from inside the folds of his kimono.*

lifetime," he joyfully exclaimed, and on the twenty-fifth day of the twelfth month, he packed his bags and left the small village of Hachiman in Omi Province for the return trip to the Capital.

Along the way, he had the good fortune of meeting and joining up with a fellow traveler also making his way up to the Capital, a young agent who worked for a wholesaler and who was carrying a large amount of money. After all, what could be more secure than traveling with someone transporting funds? While on their way, they stopped in the town of Kusatsu at a spot called Yagura, which was famous for a dish called "granny rice-cakes." Yagura was also where the main road forked, with one branch leading to a dock in Yabase for travelers who wished to proceed to the Capital by ship, and the other branch leading to Seta for those who preferred an overland route.

The two rested for a spell in an intimate teahouse where they enjoyed the surroundings. With not a cloud in the sky to spoil their view of Mount Kagami, no wind rustling the pines, and a perfectly still sea, Jimbei's companion suggested that if ever there was a day fit for traveling by ship, then surely today was such a day. But Jimbei did not agree.

"Please go ahead and take whichever way you like, but I'm going to take the land route. And if you really want to know why, I'll tell you. I value my life, and since a man has only one, I'm not about to climb into some risky little boat, especially when I'm carrying a lot of money."

And so Jimbei settled on the overland route via Seta. The young agent from the wholesaler's was rather put off by Jimbei's remarks and said, "You and I have come quite a way together to get this far, and now what do you have to worry about on a day like today? I'm carrying three hundred *ryo* with me, and I'm going to take the ship. What's the difference between your situation and mine? Well, an important man with lots of money has to be careful, so take care and watch over yourself." And with these words he stood up and set off for the dock at Yabase.

The proprietor of the teahouse, who had overheard bits of the exchange, came up to Jimbei and said, "Why would someone who always travels by ship be so concerned with the weather as fine as it is today?"

"Since I've been awfully lucky this time around," replied Jimbei, "and since I've made sixty or so *me*, I'm going to be extra careful, and under no circumstances will I set foot in a boat!" And so, ever so prudently, he set off for Seta.

Although he could have hired a horse to take him as far as Otsu, he chose instead to walk—just to be on the safe side. The twilight bell of the Ishiyama Temple was just tolling as he was passing through the Awazu moor when two men who looked to be masterless samurai jumped out of a grove of pines and said, "We know you're going to find this heartless, but it's a difficult time of year for all of us, and just give a thought to how desperate we must be. All we ask for is what we need for the New Year," and with these words they poked their hands into his baggage. Since his pleas for mercy fell on deaf ears, Jimbei did what he had to and handed over the silver from inside the folds of his kimono. The two scoundrels got away with eighty *me*, and the rest of Jimbei's trip was rather lonely and gloomy, to say the least, with little for him to do but lament his misfortune.

"No matter how hard I may work and slave to make a living," Jimbei thought to himself, "it looks as though I'll never make it back to that two-hundred-*me* mark." To this day he is still working at it.

• 5 • The hozu river and a millionaire from yamazaki

If we count back from now, in the early spring of 1689, two million three hundred and thirty-six thousand two hundred and eighty-three years have passed since the time of the Sun Goddess Amaterasu, and for all these years our country has enjoyed great prosperity. But still more impressive is the way the pine tree that symbolizes our majesty's rule goes on and on into the future. There are other examples, too. There will always be a Mount Fuji, just as there has always been a P'eng-lai in China, and east of the Never-Aging Gate of the Imperial Palace we see that the brilliant moonbeams of the full moon over Mushashino moor are different from those in foreign skies. The branches of trees on Maple Hill in the imperial compound are colored with the tints of a thousand autumns, and in the deep seas around Edo there is a turtle that has lived peacefully for ten thousand years beneath the waveless waters.

Edo is the home of merchants who perform services for the government, families like the Kitamura, Naraya, and

Taruya. Then there are administrators from all the great cities. At one time or another they all make their homes here, as do those who mint our gold and silver coins and print the vermilion bills. And one should also mention shipping magnates with certificates of passage valid throughout the country, and others whose names anyone will recognize. Yes, these are men who bring dignity to the merchant's profession and whose accomplishments can be held up like mirrors to inspire us all.

In our own times, the Saga Suminokura family from the Capital has flourished, and now they are virtually millionaires. What is more, the family has over twenty beautiful children. Their fortune had its start when Suminokura Ryoi, the builder and excavator, dedicated the first bridge over the Takase Canal, in whose currents flowed the celebrated life-prolonging waters of the Iwai Springs. The clearance of the bridge was high enough to allow the passage of good-sized cargo vessels carrying grains and firewood to the Capital. These proved a great boon to all in the metropolis and brought prosperity to many a hearth.

Another instance of how the Suminokura family helped others concerns the Hozu River. Suminokura Ryoi dredged a channel through more than two leagues of rapids past Mount Kame in Tamba and as far as Saga, thus for the first time making the river safe for navigation. Nowadays ships pass up and down its waters with ease, and captains effortlessly maneuver away from dangerous rocks and bends as their ships safely pass along the swift currents and cascading waters. With Mount Atago to the left and the hill of Oinosaka to the right, the view from this ravine so close to the Capital is comparable to that of the famed island of Matsushima.

Once upon a time there lived a businessman in the

environs of the Takara Temple in Yamazaki who made his living selling lamp oil while traveling on the distant mountain circuit. One day he was riding down the Hozu River in one of the very boats I have just been describing, and as the boat reached a particularly steep ravine known as Monkey's Leap, great swarms of monkeys all in a pack and far too numerous to count started crossing the river. Two of these filthy creatures were carrying branches full of chestnuts. Just as the merchant noticed that these two monkeys were finding it impossible to cross over, a hunter came from around the bend.

When the hunter aimed his gun, the monkey in front fell to the ground screaming and pointing his finger to show the monkey behind that something was wrong. The hunter, thinking that the monkey in front was gesturing at him to take aim at the one behind, laughed and said, "Do you really think that's going to help you?" and fired his rifle. Alas, both monkeys fell on the spot, but when the hunter came close to look over his game, he saw that though one of the monkeys had been shot dead on target, the other appeared to be uninjured and was holding a stick more than a foot long in his little hand. Thinking this odd, the hunter took a closer look and saw that the poor monkey was blind. When he saw the monkey weeping profusely and wailing over the body of his dead companion, the hunter realized that the dead monkey must have been the blind one's son.

While he paused to think about how the dead monkey must have exerted all his efforts for his father and the many years he must have cared for him, he flagged down the ship passing by. The passengers aboard all agreed that this was a most pitiable state of affairs. Since the hunter intended to beat the blind monkey to death, the salesman from Yamazaki bought the monkey for two hundred *mon* and took him home with him. For over two years he tended to the poor beast and genuinely sympathized with his plight.

As the year drew to a close, this seller of lamp oil found himself short of the funds needed to settle his year-end debts. Handing over his few remaining possessions to his creditors, he secretly concluded discussions with his wife for a declaration of bankruptcy. The next morning, the twenty-seventh day of the twelfth month, the decision was made to abandon the premises late that evening. His wife approached the monkey and spoke to him as one would speak to a human: "It is a floating, uncertain world we live in, and so we've wound up like this. At times like these, most people would abandon even their only child, so we're going to leave you behind in the house. Please don't hold it against us." Then, to get the monkey through until the spring, she put enough food into a satchel, together with some beans left over from the Bean-Scattering Festival and some unpolished rice.

In the middle of the night, the couple made their final preparations for departure. They wrapped their child inside the frame of the *kotatsu* footwarmer, a small pot went into a bag to be hung from a shoulder pole, and various other bags were stuffed with wheat and red beans and other odds and ends. The wife opened up the household Buddhist altar and took out her rosary beads and carried them by hand. Then she put on her wicker hat which, in woman's style, had the crown removed, and finally made her farewell to the house that had once been their home.

"I wonder who'll live here next?" she mused. "When you think about it, it's a fine tub of pickles we find ourselves in, for I never dreamed it would come to this. Last summer I pickled cucumbers and eggplants in salty water knowing how you like to eat salty things, but now it's just so much

One day he was riding down the Hozu River . . . and as the boat reached a particularly steep ravine known as Monkey's Leap, great swarms of monkeys all in a pack and far too numerous to count started crossing the river. Two of these filthy creatures were carrying branches full of chestnuts. . . . A hunter came from around the bend. . . . The monkey in front fell to the

SOME FINAL WORDS OF ADVICE · 80

ground screaming and pointing his finger to show the monkey behind that something was wrong. The hunter, thinking that the monkey in front was gesturing at him to take aim at the one behind, laughed and said, "Do you really think that's going to help you?" and fired his rifle.

wasted water. But I suppose you can't have everything." She took one last look through her empty cupboards and knocked over the jar of tooth-blackening dye. "The more I look, the sadder it all becomes. Please let's be on our way!" she said, weeping. Her husband joined her in her tears.

"It looks like it's a heartless world we live in," he said. "They say that even these days, commercial houses will loan merchants in the Capital eighteen thousand *kamme* without interest and with as long as ten years to repay. According to our household account books, we spend a total of seven *kan* seven hundred and sixty-two *mon* each year just on bean curd, so there are considerable expenses involved in keeping a household. If we only had enough money to pay just our bills for bean curd I could grow old in peace. But oh, what's the use!"

Just as they were about to make their getaway, the blind monkey came up to the wife and let out a shriek while tugging at the hem of her skirt. When, as if to say good-bye to a human, she turned to take one last look at his face, the monkey pulled an ornamental sword-hilt carved in the shape of a tiger from out of his mouth and handed it to her.

Her husband looked at it and realized that it was a genuine antique worth at least three *momme* of gold. "How happy you've made us by your kindness," he exclaimed. "Long ago when the great dance master Kowaka was proceeding up to the Capital from his native Echizen, he came upon a pack of monkeys deep in the mountains. They danced for him, and as a reward for their kindness he gave them a sword. Known as the Monkey Sword, it had been handed down in the Kowaka family from generation to generation. That the monkey has now given us this treasure is proof that we have acted in accord with the Heavenly Way. With this I can pay all our year-end bills!"

And so the man and woman changed their plans and dropped all their talk of late-night escapes. He sold the piece for cash and paid off a little to each of his creditors. He also dressed in new outfits and ended the year by putting New Year's pine decorations on the gate to his home. In the following year he was conscientious in his business, and from then on he and his family steadily prospered until he eventually had his own business selling lamp oil. The gods have always shone their grace upon the head of an honest man. He also began producing fine-quality hair oil, you see, and when the oil he gave as an offering to the god Sekido Myojin was burned at the shrine, there was not the slightest blemish in the vapors or shadows.

Within fourteen or fifteen years he became a millionaire in Yamazaki. His storehouse was filled with countless treasures, and he came to realize that if ever there was a magic mallet that could make one's wishes come true, then surely it was the mallet he used to extract lamp oil in his home. The way he made his millions could be compared to the valiant way a camphor tree grows—slowly but steadily upward.

His only son was now sixteen years old. In order to impart to the young man some knowledge of how to earn a living, his father presented him with a plain shingle normally used for carrying a folding-fan box he had received one New Year's. On the shingle were two one-*mon* coins. "Let's see," said his father, "if you can use your wits to do some business with this as your capital." The son pondered these words for some time, and with one of the coins he bought some paper and with the other coin he bought paste. Then he glued the paper to the shingle his father had given him, drew a black star on it, and showed it to his father as a target for rifle shooting. But his father did not approve of the lad's efforts and advised him, "I doubt that you'll find a market for this. Do this: Split what you have there in two and sell it as facing for a trouser skirt." His son took the suggestion to heart, went up to the Capital, called on a haberdasher, made his very first sale for six *mon,* and returned home. This marked the start of his acquiring a fortune by using his wits.

A young man succeeding at making a living by using a present of cash from his parents is exactly the same as a samurai warrior living off his hereditary stipend. If a person were to save just one *mon* each day from the day he was born, after one hundred days the money could be deposited in a bank at ten percent interest, and after sixty years he would have sixty *kamme.* When you stop to think about it in these terms, there is no excuse for not making every effort to economize.

The son thought to himself, "If it's really true that I can earn interest just by loaning out money, what could be better!" And when his savings added up to one *kamme,* he left his home in Yamazaki, thereby giving up all claims to inheritance, and returned to the Capital, where he consulted a bank specializing in loaning money to needy daimyo. By depositing his money in the care of this enterprise, he was able to loan out his one *kamme* at twelve percent annual interest, and by redepositing his earnings for thirty years, he found himself in possession of a tidy fortune of twenty-nine *kan* nine hundred and fifty-nine *momme* eight *fun* four *rin* and one *mo*. He then withdrew the money from the bank, put it into a chest, and eventually managed to loan it out himself. Before long he had one thousand *kamme*. From then on he made money more and more rapidly until by the time he died he had accumulated the grand sum of seven thousand *kamme*, and his name was even entered into the social register of the thirty-six richest men in the Capital.

The way this man took one shingle and two one-*mon* coins from his father and turned them as I have described into a millionaire's fortune should serve as an example, just like a mirror, of what a merchant can do in this world. If you look at number twenty-eight in the Kyoto Register and see the name Yamazaki, this is the man to whom it refers. His descendants carried on the family name and tradition for generation after generation, ending each year by placing pine decorations on the gates to their homes and having the pleasure of greeting many, many felicitous springtimes.

• 6 • A mother-in-law's instructions after the honeymoon

When interest rates are only six percent, there is no investment sounder than taking a mortgage on a large house, renting it out, and using the rental income as your mortgage payment. Of course, there is always the worry of loss due to fire, but such things do not really happen more than, oh, once in a century, and in fourteen years one can pay off the mortgage and still have the property as a treasure for countless years to come. In recent years, though, even if a wealthy man acquires a house in his own name, there are still many difficulties in managing its rental. So instead, for him, it is much better if he takes the sum of, say, one hundred *kamme*, pays the title tax on a house with it, and then, having loaned someone whatever it takes to actually buy the house, acts as the landlord. Not only does he have the signature seals of the ward officials and the five-family association* on the title to the property, but the rent received

---

* A five-family association (*gonin-gumi*) was the smallest unit of local administration in Saikaku's day. It comprised five households who con-

from the property guarantees repayment of the loan; it makes this one very secure way of loaning something.

All sorts of pressures bear upon the borrower. Moreover, since none of these transactions is in any way private, there is no way the borrower can keep his personal affairs under wraps and maintain appearances in the neighborhood. If one were to say just who can benefit from such an arrangement, then it is the man who wishes to order a shipment of rice from the Western Provinces and set up a new wholesaling operation, or the man who agrees to act as guarantor for another's loan, or perhaps the man who comes from the countryside and needs a dowry in order to become an adopted son, or even the man entertaining thoughts of getting married—in other words, men who need to create the secure impression of being householders in order to settle a deal without a hitch.

Nowadays when people marry, the go-betweens are generally entitled to one tenth of the dowry, but more often than not they seem to swindle you out of half of it. When the parents of the bride tell lies, their deceit is usually something on the order of having their daughter wear kimonos with long, hanging sleeves until the age of twenty-two or twenty-three because these clothes make her look as if she were just going on eighteen. This, after all, is not such a terrible lie.

The deceits that take place on the groom's side are quite another matter. One young man took a short-term loan in order to provide his fiancée with the customary engagement gifts of silk scrolls and "wrapped money" and made all the wedding preparations himself. No sooner did he receive the dowry money than he used it to pay off the bearers of credit notes who were snapping at his heels. By the time the newly-

---

sulted on matters pertaining to their immediate neighborhood and who also shared responsibility for the transgressions of any one member.

weds returned from their five-day honeymoon, the husband had proved himself to be crude in just about everything.

On the honeymoon's last day he informed the housemaid and seamstress that from then on they would only be hired when needed, complained that their wedding presents were skimpy, and left his wife to make the courtesy visit to her family's home by herself. When he entered a confectionery to pick up some cedar boxes of sweets for his wife to take home as presents, they told him there that his accounts were still in arrears from long before and that there would be no further extension of credit. In the fish store it was much the same story, for the owner falsely claimed to be out of the red snapper he wanted. Finally the groom managed to trick the proprietor of a stationery shop and sent his wife home with presents of Sugihara paper for everyone. But by the time she arrived, the bride's lady-in-waiting and nurse had returned home and had told her mother all the details of the disastrous honeymoon.

"Well, young lady," admonished her mother, "I expect that you will show some common sense by going and fetching your things before it's too late."

If there is any single grief attached to being a woman, then this is it—once she's married, it is the end of her freedom. Since a divorce would not reflect well on her family, they decided not to breathe a word to anyone, and as the time approached to prepare for the young lady's departure, her mother gave her the following instructions:

"As for the dowry money, there's nothing we can do about that. If he asks to borrow your clothing or furniture and puts them into hock, that's the last you'll ever see of them. Just tell him, 'I have to ask my mother at home before I can agree to anything,' and don't lend him a single kimono. If his mother should give you a hard time, just wrap, unobserved, two or three of your finer articles in a *furoshiki* each time you return here for a visit. In a few trips you'll have emptied your closets, and then you can follow through with your scheme for the actual divorce. But if you get pregnant during this time then there'll be trouble. As long as you don't have any children you can always marry someone else.

"The way to kill this man's affection is simple—stay in bed all morning and don't fix your hair; say that you're exhausted and that getting up makes you dizzy; sleep during the day, too, and never have anything to say; always act ill on the first and last days of the month when people expect you to be pleasant; say that grilled meats and fish salad don't taste right and poke disinterestedly at your food; ask for broth and gruel or anything else troublesome to prepare when your husband is in a hurry; act silly when family and friends are visiting; and every three days announce that you're going to visit your mother—after a while you'll find that this is enough to make any man fed up.

"And when you and he finally have words with each other, that is the time to say, 'It's wrong for you to have to sit and look at any woman for even one day who does not suit your fancy. Wouldn't it be better if we made a complete break of things? There's no shortage of girls in the world and there must be any number of young ladies who would be just right for you. I've gotten fat and I'm not much to look at, so I'll just take the ten *kamme* that I brought here as my dowry and the house in the suburbs with the sixty-foot frontage and, oh yes, the storehouse down by the beach with all the valuables I inherit when father passes away. With my house and money I should manage all right.' If you say all this in your most willful tone of voice, by my word, then we'll have our chance.

"But if he should prove reluctant to strike the first blow, then I want you to cut off the ends of your lovely black hair and fling them at him, scream so loudly that all the neighbors hear, and then, when a crowd begins to form, pack off for home just as you are. As your parent, my main advice to you ought to be 'Give your household priority,' but if I tell you something so nasty as 'Get rid of the fellow and come back home!' it's because that young man is good for nothing. It is most important for a woman to know about these things, so don't forget a single word that your mother has told you, dear."

The daughter felt that what her mother had told her made perfect sense, and, taking the words to heart, she returned to her husband's house. But with each night she and her husband spent together, they came to feel more and more tenderly toward each other, and the daughter realized that no matter what her mother might think about the situation, it was neither natural nor right for a woman to change husbands. She disregarded her mother's advice and showed no dismay when she was discreetly removed from the family will and disowned. She became a devoted wife, and it never bothered her that she and her husband had nothing left but the skin on their backs. As is so often the case in this world of ours, they took their medicine and tried to make the best of the situation.

One by one, her old short-sleeved kimonos, reminders of better days, were pawned. When everyone wore light, unlined summer kimonos, she and her husband wore old ones with linings, and at those times when others wore clothing with cotton padding as insulation from the cold, they had only unpadded garments to protect them from the blustery winds. Finally, in the wife's appearance there remained not the faintest hint of her former worldly elegance.

As in just about all things, it is only later that we really understand what we should have done. A man who for year after year has had but the most meager livelihood told me that when he first became poor he sought relief by putting his things into hock. But since he was never able to settle his accounts with the pawn shop once and for all, it would have been far better had he tried to tide himself over by selling his articles outright for whatever price they might have fetched at the time. The years pass by, and what is really terrifying is how quickly the interest piles up in a pawn shop.

Each year, the man would pawn one high-quality but quite worn hempen jacket and one brown, patterned jacket made from Kaga silk, and for these two articles he would get some seven *momme* five *fun*. He would put them into hock each autumn and take them out the following summer, at which time he would pay back the initial amount he borrowed plus whatever interest he had been charged. And so by putting these things in and out of hock year after year for nineteen years, he paid out a total of seventeen *momme* one *fun* in interest. It has recently reached the point where he no longer gets from the pawnshop as much for these goods as he used to. But even though he now receives only five *momme* five *fun* for all his trouble, he continues to put these things into hock.

Now let us consider what happens when a man mortgages his home. If a man has come across some sound business enterprise and is only using the mortgage money to finance the venture, this is one thing. But one man I know lived in a house whose extra room had provided rental income to support his family from the time he was a child, and no sooner did he inherit the property than he mortgaged it in order to effect various unnecessary improvements and to indulge in various extravagances beyond his means. These proved the death of his finances. As long as the man was living just like his neighbors and paying for the food on his table, he had nothing to fear. But when he sought official approval for the mortgage from the local authorities he had to pander to the five-family association and the ward officials, and by that time the attitude of those in the neighborhood toward him had changed. Even local magistrates no longer squatted quite as low while they spoke with him as they did for others, and the barber, too, no longer had an appointment for him when he wanted one. All of this resulted in one embarrassment after another.

Old friends came as before to invite him to go flower-viewing or sightseeing, but somehow he no longer felt up to their company. He even shied from telling stories that he knew perfectly well, and he felt awkward in his dealings with others. Since he never gave a thought to how he was going to pay back the money after mortgaging his house, the unpaid interest was added to the original debt, changing the terms of the contract. As the years passed, the situation reached the point where even if he were to sell the house, every last penny would go to pay off the mortgage. When the term of the mortgage elapsed, he was hounded by the realtor, and since he repeatedly made a nuisance of himself by calling on people in the neighborhood to help him out of this dilemma, even those who had originally been sympathetic to his situation and who had been on intimate terms with him for many years now wanted nothing to do with him. They even informed the realtor of his pressed circumstances and advised him to foreclose on the mortgage as soon as possible.

When, with no other choice open to him, the man signed over the house to his creditors, his aged mother was particularly distressed and said: "Your parents built this home before there was a single well in the neighborhood, and for two generations it was perfectly adequate without any of these so-called improvements. We used a six-inch ridge pole to hold up the house, and this sturdy beam stood us in good stead until this very year. Whenever people came to draw water from our well, I had them address me as 'My Lady' and squat low before me. If we attended a tea ceremony, we were always given seats of honor. Thanks to your late father, we were praised to the skies. But I suppose this is what one should expect from an only child, that due to your absurd stubbornness, now that I have one foot in the grave, we should be in such a fix.

"I thought that if I had a funeral my final departure from our house would be showered in flowers, and the high doorsill on the inner door was expressly designed to let the funeral caisson pass under it without obstruction. Can you ever understand my sadness in parting from a house to which we have devoted so much time and attention?"

The old woman went into the kitchen to take one last look at the empty cupboards and pulled down a rack from which her kitchen ladles had once hung. In the garden it was the season for the stately plum trees to shed their blossoms, and this likewise moved her to add painfully, "Each year in the fifth month we gathered two bushels of plums but when I think of it, it's just too sad," and she shook several branches, causing the petals to fall to the ground. "Let this tree wither from being watered by my tears," she concluded.

Her words may sound unreasonable, but they were perfectly natural coming from a woman's heart. Considering how difficult it must have been to part from her home, one cannot help but sympathize with her feelings, since this

Thinking that at least he might pick up some rice cakes, he rapped on the door of a shop and called out, "I want to buy rice cakes!" Though his knocking caused the rats lying about to scatter every which way, inside it looked as if both the owner and his wife were sound asleep.

bitter experience was brought upon her by the poor judgment of her only child.

However, a man's fortune has nothing to do with whether he is particularly wise or clever; it hinges on fate and opportunity. After this man was forced to close up his house, he set out for other parts and by hard work managed to double his former earnings, so that in the end he was able to bedeck his wife in brocades and fulfill their most longstanding desires. If a man clings to his wife and is afraid to set off on his own when the time calls for it, people will point at him and snicker, for it isn't in human nature to be content with a meager living.

In those days, too, there was a businessman in the Nishihama section of Osaka who for many years had worked both conscientiously and singlemindedly at earning a living. Though he tried his hand at all sorts of ventures, they never did as well as he might have wished. "Before my affairs turn for the worse," he thought to himself, "perhaps I should set off for distant parts to find a spot where a man can make a living. After all, a man's only comfort in his old age is silver and gold." And so he resolved to go out and seek his fortune.

Since the Chugoku area was so close to home, he found things there unpromising. He traveled all through Kyushu and finally wound up at the foot of the castle in Satsuma. Having used up most of his money in the course of this long trip, he did not even have enough to pay for a room for the night. A place called Daishoji was in the business district of Izumi and close to the docks, and there at all hours of the day and night were lanterns burning in house after house to indicate where rice, *miso* broth, and salt were sold, as well as those inns whose keepers were not yet asleep. Thinking that at least he might pick up some rice cakes, he rapped on the door of a shop and called out, "I want to buy rice cakes!"

Though his knocking caused the rats lying about to scatter every which way, inside it looked as if both the owner and his wife were sound asleep. But the shop owner's wife, who had heard him, asked, "How many do you want?"

"I'd like five *mon*'s worth, please," he replied.

This time the owner himself called out saying, "Look, we've been sleeping and we don't get up for orders of just five or ten *mon*."

After hearing this, the poor man did not even bother to reply. "Well, well," he thought, "this certainly looks like a port where hard work could pay off. If they can't bother to fill five- or ten-*mon* orders of rice cakes, I imagine there's more than enough business to go around." He decided that this would be a good place to settle down. As the years passed, he worked day after day at his fortune, and from a humble business selling lantern oil he acquired some capital. Because his house steadily prospered, he firmly believed that it was all due to the blessings of the gods and Buddhas, and daily he journeyed to pray to the gods of Gion enshrined in a place called Tanoura.

The scenery of this coastal town, with its different trees and rocky crags, was truly exceptional, and people spoke of the area as a favorite abode of hermits since ancient times. One evening when he was visiting the shrine, a young girl fourteen or fifteen years old and very beautiful approached him and handed him a bolt of old-looking silk that she had pulled from the folds of her kimono. "This is all I can use to support my mother," she said, "so please take it and pay me whatever you wish for it."

He felt compassion for her and said, "Please, that won't

One evening when he was visiting the shrine, a young girl fourteen or fifteen years old and very beautiful approached him and handed him a bolt of old-looking silk. . . . "This is all I can use to support my mother," she said, "so please take it and pay me whatever you wish for it."

be necessary," and handed her the more than twenty *momme* he was carrying at the time.

"I cannot accept your money without giving something in return," she said, and insistently placed the bolt of silk before him and departed. Since there was nothing else that he could do, he took the silk and went home. When he showed it to people with an eye for such things, they told him that it was an extremely rare example of an ancient Chinese weave called the Little Vine. After hearing this he went back and tried to learn where the girl was living, but since she could not be found, he came to think of the silk as a reward from one of the young ladies of the Gion Shrine. After selling it to a man from the Capital for eighty gold coins, he eventually grew to be a very wealthy man. His four sons all established themselves in different ways, and his own enterprise was known far and wide as "the oil shop where never a drop was spilt." Aside from valuables and precious objects, his retirement savings totaled three thousand *kamme* in cash. Everyone knew the story of his family's having moved from Osaka to start a new life, and the fact that he had accomplished all this in his lifetime should serve as an example to all his fellow merchants.

It is particularly when a man takes honesty as his principle that his later success is due to fate and good fortune. When you stop to think about it, it is just not natural for a man who knows the ways of business to be careless and lose his livelihood and end up sharing his roof with the God of Poverty. Please, do think it over.

• 7 • A modern-day kusunoki masashige

Next door to the great writer Yoshida Kenko there lived a man named Enokibara Nobumichi who served with Lord Yoshida in the palace guard of the Emperor Go-uda. Perhaps it was due to his service in the Imperial Palace, but even into his fifties the gentleman remained ignorant of the fact that copper coins had writing on both sides. Nor did he have any idea of how to hold a poem card right side up. This man, who could not properly be called either courtier or commoner, spent his days and nights playing *go* so intently that he lost all sense of time until the eve of the New Year, when he would find irate bill collectors pounding at his door.

People who lack proper foresight encountered the same troubles in that long-ago age that they do now. Lord Yoshida has left a splendid account of the agitated state of the man who pretends not to be at home when the bill collector, brandishing a pine torch through the long night, raps at the door and announces, "It's the liquor store, sir."* We still have receipts from the time Musashi-no-Bo Benkei borrowed five bushels of horse fodder in Amagasaki and also from the time Ise-no-Saburo Yoshimori loaned five hundred *kamme* to the farmers of Saga. Both these men were in the service of Minamoto Yoshitsune. Benkei enjoyed a generous stipend, but since he insisted on always carrying seven superfluous pieces of equipment, he never had any money. People say that it was because Yoshimori had such a keen sense of economy that he always had a good livelihood.

It is a fact of life in this world that there will always be some who are wealthy and others who are poor. Long ago in the Capital, there was a family enterprise known as the Kichimonjiya, and for many years two clerks worked in this shop. Year after year these clerks worked both within and without the shop, in selfless dedication to their employer, and as a consequence of their travails (though some would have us believe that it was due to the good fortune of the owner), the account books at the end of one year showed the grand sum of ten thousand *kamme* in ready cash. This they happily showed their employer when the figures were transferred into new books for the first month.

Now since it had been a long-standing dream of the owner that he should one day tally ten thousand *kamme*, he could think of nothing that he might have wanted more and was overjoyed at the news. He assigned the duties of the two

---

* This is from Chapter 19 of Yoshida Kenko's *Tsurezuregusa*. Kenko (1294–1350) was a courtier of the late Kamakura period who achieved considerable fame as a poet and essayist. The *Tsurezuregusa*, his best-known work, is a miscellany of personal thoughts, reflections, and anecdotes intended to guide the reader to an honorably elegant life; it has been translated by Donald Keene under the title *Essays in Idleness* (New York: Columbia University Press, 1967).

SOME FINAL WORDS OF ADVICE · **100**

employees to junior clerks and decided that the first order of business was to get both of them new homes and arrange their schedules so they could work on alternate days. He went so far as to have their houses built in fine locations, and on top of that he gave them each two hundred *kamme*, which each used to open a bank. Since handling money was something in which they both had considerable experience, neither ever reported the loss of a single penny, whether in making loans, buying up gold coins, or trying to unload copper coin reserves.

Their becoming wealthy after years of service was by no means due exclusively to their cleverness; rather, it was all thanks to the kindness of the employer who had given them the money by which they got their start. One of the two clerks accumulated the small fortune of five hundred *kamme* within less than ten years, but the other lived out his days without ever increasing his original stake of two hundred *kamme*. When the stories of these two reached the ears of the battery of clerks who were still working in the Kichimonjiya shop, they snickered at the news, saying, "Hah! They may have started out with the same money, but look what happened because of the different ways they used it!"

Their employer learned about this and said, "Why, you fools! You've been maligning a man wise in the ways of making a living! It's precisely because he's the kind of man he is that he has been able to make it up to now without losing any of the original two hundred *kamme*. Let me tell you, when the man who made the five hundred *kamme* struck off on his own, his luck held up and there were no obstacles for him to overcome. But the other clerk, from the day he started, ran into the kinds of expense no man could have predicted, and this is where he got into trouble.

As far as I'm concerned, your criticism of his circumstances shows your utter stupidity.

"Ever since the evening he proposed to his wife, this man knew, sad as it might sound, that if he married a woman with expensive tastes he would never make his fortune, no matter how hard he worked. As you well know, his father-in-law was a well-established gentleman with some eight hundred *kamme*. The girl herself was young and was the talk of the town because of her good looks. He knew then that he had a host of undreamed-of expenses on his hands. Since his father-in-law loaned his money at ten percent interest throughout the year, he was an 'eighty *kamme*' man, but his son-in-law realized he would never be more than a 'twenty *kamme*' man. It was like trying for a victory when you're badly outnumbered. Even though he eventually had to retreat, in business tactics he was no less a soldier than any Kusunoki Masashige.* Wouldn't he have made a fine commander just by virtue of his holding down the fort and not losing any of the original money?"

When the clerks heard this they said, "A man like you who can make a fortune of ten thousand *kamme* in one lifetime is truly the most splendid commander. He has wisdom, he has devotion, and he has courage!" and they one and all served their master faithfully like warriors before a great commander.

---

* A general of near-legendary prowess on the battlefield. His reputation was enhanced by his loyalty to the Emperor Godaigo during the civil wars that rocked Japan in the 1330s.

• 8 • Mr. happiness, the salt vendor

In the vicinity of the Shimmei Shrine in Kyoto's Awataguchi district there was an old, isolated cottage whose roof came down so low that one could reach up and touch the bamboo thatch at the edge of its eaves, and in this cottage lived an elderly couple. Now this man and his wife, sad to say, had no children, though both were in their sixties. The woman did the work of a man, manufacturing horseshoes that she then displayed on the bamboo shutter of her window and sold to packdrivers on their way to Otsu. In this way she helped make ends meet at home.

Each day her husband went up to the Capital, where he had a small business selling packaged quantities of salt. In this way he made it from one day to the next with never a thought of what tomorrow might bring. When he came home at the end of the day he would light the fire with clover brushwood gathered at the meadows of Kurusuno and dine on taros from Yamashina washed down with tea picked at the Kanju Temple. He was perfectly content with these simple pleasures and bore no grudges against those in the world who were blessed with money or fame.

His life throughout the year was rather like a dream—on the one hand there was not the pounding of rice balls in the first month or the trays of mackerel during the Festival of All Souls or the thoughts of bowls of chestnuts or chrysanthemum wine as the Festival in the Ninth Month neared; but on the other hand no man owed him for credit sales, and likewise he had no bills of his own to settle. While his humble existence might have appeared trying from the outside, the truth of the matter is that he was a veritable Mr. Happiness inside his own home.

Now it was about the eighth day of the ninth month, the day which you and I know as the eve of the Chrysanthemum Festival, a day when the sound of scurrying feet is more frantic than usual. On this busy day even the woman who usually wore clothes dyed in the classical hues of the imperial court dashed about the streets indifferent to her own appearance and to what people might think of her.

The flurry of activity around a house some thirty or thirty-five yards long that belonged to one of the drapers in the Nakadachiuri area suggested that today was the occasion for the raising of the ridgepole. Workers were beating curtains; the beauty of the gold-leafed screens vied with that of the carpets; in the storeroom men were unloading casks of wine and boxes of fish faster than they could be checked off in the household account books; and in the kitchen servants were receiving their instructions for the festivities. With the ladies of the family like so many flowers all dressed in their finest and the menfolk hovering around trays of food decorated to suggest the P'eng-lai Isle of Eternal Youth, the banquet began.

There was an old, isolated cottage whose roof came down so low that one could reach up and touch the bamboo thatch at the edge of its eaves, and in this cottage lived an elderly couple. . . . The woman did the work of a man, manufacturing horseshoes that she then displayed on the bamboo shutter of her window and sold to packdrivers on their way to Otsu.

There were various professional entertainers and no end to the laughter as everyone enjoyed the performances enormously—especially after the seventh round of drinks. Dressed in ceremonial headgear and robes, carpenters decorated the room with ritual stripes of white cloth and laid out bows and arrows by the northeast corner of the house, the so-called Demon Gate, in order to keep threatening spirits at bay.

Finally, with the carpenters all beating their mallets in time, the ridgepole was pounded into position as the assembled guests filled the air with cheers of "Banzai! Banzai!"

When the waiters brought the traditional five hundred and eighty rice cakes to the table, the crowding was such that even the broadest of boulevards would have seemed too narrow. Those passers-by who had no great envy for material treasures took only a look and then moved on. But those who stopped to watch the goings-on agreed to a man that only a millionaire could afford to build such a house, designed as it was to be handed down from one generation to the next, and took guesses at the value of its treasures, paying extra attention to the inner storehouse. This kind of envy, however, serves no good purpose.

Until twenty years ago the man responsible for all this had made his living by papering lanterns and was too poor even to blow out a candle. But somehow he managed to become a wealthy man. He paid attention to minor details, but his real breakthrough came when he smeared persimmon juice on mica paper and invented what we know today as the "rain lantern"; it is actually true, just as people say, that he is now worth seven thousand *kamme*. Since, in former times, even people from Kyoto would sit up and take notice as long as you had enough money and were not some country carpenter with blistered hands, this lantern maker had been able to marry a girl from one of the oldest and best families. You may be tired of hearing this, but it still bears repeating: nothing shines as brightly in this world as money.

But our old friend, the salt vendor, had not the slightest desire to build such a house, being quite content simply to have a brief look at the people dancing to songs sung by beautiful voices. He found it most amusing, but after the spectators had drifted off, he picked up an Indian-style red-striped coin purse that someone had apparently left behind. "Is the person who dropped this still here, by any chance?" he called out.

A priestly looking man of about fifty came up and said, "Oh yes, I dropped it and would like it back."

"What good luck," said the salt salesman. "I'll gladly give it back to you, but just one thing. Now I don't doubt for a minute that this is yours, but would you just tell me the contents of the purse?"

"Why there's nothing in it but some hundred *me* in small change," answered this "priest."

When he heard this the salt vendor's face flushed and his entire expression changed. "Really, how can a man your age stoop so low? The purse contains gold coins, so it couldn't be yours. If the person who dropped this is still here, please come to my house to collect it." And to avoid confusion, he went straight home.

That evening a young man came to the door and introduced himself as a clerk at the Hishiya silk shop on Muromachi Avenue in the Saigyo-zakura ward. "The purse has *koban* coins in it worth one hundred and twenty *ryo*," he began. "You see, I was carrying them back from a wholesaler in the Western Provinces. . . ." He then went on to explain how his employer's livelihood would suffer without the money.

Our old friend . . . had not the slightest desire to build such a house, being quite content simply to have a brief look at the people dancing. . . . After the spectators had drifted off, he picked up an Indian-style red-striped coin purse that someone had apparently left behind. "Is the person who dropped this still here, by any chance?" he called out.

When he finished his story, the salt salesman said, "You are quite right. The wallet has exactly one hundred and twenty *ryo* worth of coins in it," and without the slightest twinge of regret he gave it back to the young man. The clerk burst into tears and could not stop weeping with joy.

"If this had fallen into other hands," he said, "surely I would never have seen it again. I'm afraid that I must be off for Kyoto again, but thanks to you, my second trip will be happier than the first!" Then he reached into the purse and tried to hand the old man five *ryo* as an expression of his gratitude, but under no circumstances would he accept them.

"This is not your money," he said. "It belongs to your employer and you cannot give me something that rightfully belongs to him. To take anything from you would be unthinkable." Since he repeatedly refused the money, the clerk had no recourse but to take all of it and return to Kyoto.

The young man, however, did not forget this act of kindness, and from then on whenever there was a rainy, windy, or snowy day that prevented the salt vendor from going up to the Capital, he would call on various people and get each of them to buy one bushel of salt from the old man. Now the salt salesman happily thought that this must be Heaven's way of rewarding him, and he passed the rest of his days without ever learning of the efforts of the clerk.

Because his conscience had not let him forget a favor once received, the clerk's good fortune also continued. He went into business for himself and not long ago became quite a wealthy man, virtually overnight, by manufacturing short-sleeved kimonos of his own design.

Now again at this time there was a famous doctor whom everyone knew in the northern part of the Capital. Because, as is the way with celebrities, this doctor was rather full of himself and felt that dealings with the nobility were not worth his trouble, he, too, withdrew to Awataguchi, where he lived on one of the smaller side streets in a secluded villa surrounded by a fashionable hedge. Since this area was along the Tokaido highway, daimyo were always passing by on their way to and from the Capital. Thanks to the doctor's reputation there, however, the daimyo would not dare censure him even if he were to sit up high when greeting them or hum tunes in their presence.

It was around dusk and after a sudden squall that this priestly looking doctor was standing in his doorway and putting on his high clogs. When he looked out into the distance and saw the old salt salesman returning home after a day's work in the Capital, he immediately rushed back inside his house. Among a crowd of passers-by, one who noticed this thought it strange and turned to his companion, saying, "Now why should anyone be so frightened by that salt salesman?"

"That man," answered his friend, "is regarded by people in these parts as a living sage. It is considered irreverent for one to put on one's clogs before a sage, and it is this that frightened him so. Since he wasn't an acquaintance of the sage he couldn't even try to take them off, so he felt it would be better if he were not seen at all."

"But why is that man regarded as a sage?" queried his friend.

"You mean to tell me you don't know? He once found a wallet with some money in it and actually returned it to its rightful owner! I'll wager you never heard of someone else doing that in or out of the Capital! Why you wouldn't even find someone like that in all of China!"

Everyone accepted the wisdom of this and they were all quite in awe of the little salt vendor.

◆ 9 ◆ Something popular and in style

It is easier for people to spend thousands on fame and profit than it is for them to scratch their heads, but getting them to give even half a copper for charity is harder than pulling teeth. This being the case, what with people's livelihoods and professions flourishing as never before in this world of ours, if some become indifferent to the world around them and decide that they have no use for ambition or gain, then it is because they have been listening to the latest Buddhist talk. These sermons sap their energies straightaway and make them delight in nothing more than subsisting from one moment to the next. Such people have lost all desire to accomplish something for the future. No one will ever become wealthy or famous by taking such thoughts to heart. Into any businessman's home where men still pray for prosperity and gain, those who think about the transience of life or give heed to others' cries of suffering should never be allowed.

A lie told in the course of business usually implies that one has been extravagant in his use of words, and sooner or later the lie will be found out. Now among all the lacquerware shops whose portals line the streets of Edo, two in particular, the Omori and the Ogawa, have long been renowned for their attention to the quality of their wares, and over the years their reputations have steadily grown.

The proprietor of the Ogawa shop once had a meager trade in which he placed a premium on honest and straightforward dealings with his customers. The story of how he made his fortune begins on the first day of the first month in 1648, when there was a tremendously heavy snowfall, so heavy in fact that it completely blocked the streets and brought all traffic, whether pedestrian or on horseback, to a standstill.

The proprietor arose at dawn that day and boiled a large tub of water, which he then poured over the snow in front of his store to clear a space that, although not very large, was yet wide enough to encourage passers-by to tarry. Before long the swarms of people stopping in to buy their New Year's presents, *hibachi,* pots for warming sakè, rice-ball steamers, and what not, grew as large as Mount P'eng-lai, so that in this one single day he made more than fifty *ryo* in cash sales. Since Edo is truly the crossroads of the world, many new faces as well as regular customers came by to shop.

That evening a monk, looking about fifty years old and wearing hempen garments with his arms bared and a bamboo hat that, like those in old pictures of Priest Saigyo, was pushed back on his head, brushed the snow off himself and strode into the shop. He expressed interest in picking up a sakè cup. Various ones were brought out and shown to him.

Now this priest, whose appearance suggested he was something of a tippler, complained that all the cups were too small. "If there's one earthly pleasure I enjoy," he explained, "it's having a good drink. Nothing else compares.

Now this priest, whose appearance suggested he was something of a tippler, complained that all the cups were too small. "If there's one earthly pleasure I enjoy," he explained, "it's having a good drink. Nothing else compares. Don't you have that extra large cup . . . the one good drinkers in the old days referred to as the cup no man could finish?"

Don't you have that extra large cup that goes by the name Musashino, the one good drinkers in the old days referred to as the cup no man could finish?"

He was then shown a sakè cup designed to hold three-quarters of a pint, but even this was not good enough. "Every cup you show me," the priest complained, "has either a scene of some chrysanthemums or maple leaves floating in the Tatsuta River or a picture of Ise prawns drawn on it. I'm tired of looking at those old-fashioned things. Show me something new and with a little imagination in it, something popular and in style."

By now the clerk in the shop was getting a bit tired of all this and thought, "What a foolish old priest. Even if I do eventually sell him a cup, it certainly is a lot of bother." But out of embarrassment at the thought that a customer might be able to say there wasn't a single cup in the entire shop that suited his wishes, the clerk showed him an exceptionally tall cup decorated with a group of desperate beggars doing a year-end dance underneath a hanging lantern.

The priest's spirits immediately brightened and he nodded his approval. "I am really Hsing-hsing the Tippler, from the Hsing-yang River area in China. I am visiting your land in my astral body, but please, do not be afraid, for I bring prosperity to any place I enter." With these words he picked up and left.

The clerk was not convinced by what he had heard, and secretly followed this Hsing-hsing, watching him from some distance behind. In the vicinity of Tsukiji the priest quietly slipped inside a small hermitage and performed various austerities that clearly showed him to be a holy man. The clerk's doubt of Hsing-hsing's words was dispelled, and it seemed to him that the shop's proprietor had been rewarded by Heaven for his honesty and straightforwardness.

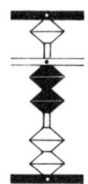

Part Two

People's Hearts in This World of Ours

◆ ◆ ◆ Author's Preface

The wind may have no body to call its own, and yet it echoes through the pine forests. On the other hand, a flower, as long as it has its colors, need not say a word to make itself felt. When I was just a child, I heard it said that things which pass before a man's eyes have a way of drifting into his mind, and unless he mentions them, they will expand and give him a swelled head. Now, I haven't had a respectable thought in ages, and for that matter, I never had a swelled head either, but what I *have* done is take these clumsy observations of people's follies and write them down, giving them the name *People's Hearts in This World of Ours*. Just like some fine twill damask imported from Cathay, I have spun these tales and woven my humble yarns.

—SAIKAKU

Osaka, a day in a month
in the Genroku (1688–1704)

• 10 • Reeling in a compliant old badger

The reign of our ruling family is as enduring as the never-changing hue of those celebrated pines that grace Mount Millennium. With the spring breezes stilled and not a ripple upon the four seas, the spell of peace pervades our land. The manners and customs of our people, whether it be the woodsman deep in the mountains who sells ferns and laurel or the shore dweller who earns his fare by selling gulfweed and herring roe, all have a certain poetic elegance about them. The Way prevailing in this land of ours is as vast and as varied as the countless particles of sand that one passes during years of travel along the seaside. It is a mark of good fortune, indeed, that we live in such a prosperous age.

In fact, when you look at the overall appearance of people these days, there is not a single one who looks dull or stupid. In former times not one in ten had the slightest notion of how things should be done, and a person who knew how to make a proper living was a rarity. Rarer still was anyone with a gift for words who could express himself clearly when acting as guarantor for another or when dealing in matters of litigation or in private settlements. But it was also unthinkable for people then greedily to seek profits for themselves by bringing charges against others, by drawing up documents without a shred of truth in them, or by inflicting untold miseries on each other. Even when the complaints were perfectly justified, you simply could not find a soul for miles around who was capable of putting the facts into writing one by one just as they had occurred, whereas nowadays just about anyone can write up his own case.

No one asks for others' advice anymore and people insist on doing everything themselves. What is more, people hardly even notice when someone else gets evil notions into his head or when he brings suffering to others. And while we ourselves always know when we are in the wrong, whether it be in our business practices or in the way we borrow money, we fabricate false charges and show just how crafty a man's heart can be.

In former times there was never trouble when people borrowed money or other things. The explanation of this is that those who borrowed money for their various enterprises made certain beforehand that they had a secure plan for using the money to its greatest advantage. They borrowed only enough to finance their ventures without exceeding their means, and then, after closing these well-thought-out deals, they repaid the entire sum as well as any accrued interest.

But these days people borrow without the slightest thought, and from the very start they have no notion of ever settling their debts. Since in their own extravagance they borrowed the money just to squander it in the licensed quarters, there is no way for the money to generate enough new money to settle the loan. Consequently they bring hardship to their creditors and invent every manner of falsehood.

It is precisely because we have laws to illuminate the difference between good and evil that the element of fear enters people's minds and prevents them from behaving as willfully as they otherwise might. For example, no matter what excuse some malevolent scheme of yours prompts you to invent, nothing can save you from the obligation of returning an item you have borrowed. With this in mind, never forget, not even for a minute, that by the time you have removed your trousers after the New Year's celebration, the days and months have fallen away and the next New Year's Eve is upon you, with all new bills to pay.

Consider all the frightening things in the world. Now you would not even bother with making way for a drunk on the street, though you would likely not challenge the drawn sword of a madman. If you avoid taking walks late at night you won't meet up with highwaymen, and as long as you dispense with unreasonable notions of making a quick fortune, you will never fall prey to swindlers and con artists. But of all the frightening things you can imagine, surely there is nothing as horrifying as having one's fortune ruined and being hounded by creditors. Nothing else even comes close.

Ah, but it's a detestable world. When a man who has enjoyed good fortune in his livelihood and has also managed to build himself a fine house says something, it may well be the stupidest thing imaginable, but people will still perk up their ears and give it their fullest attention. But a pauper's words can make perfect sense and no one will pay them the slightest heed. The poor man's life is just a succession of embarrassments, and he is doubted even by people who know nothing about his subject.

Those who enjoy the blessings of wealth and fame can be at ease even in the midst of other people's wranglings over money, but the poor man, always in the background, dares not even approach loose copper change, and his heart can find no peace. No matter how fundamentally honest a man may be, if he is poor, others will be on guard when he is around, and if there are small tools or utensils within his reach people will shift them closer to themselves to keep an eye on them. Such pettiness is simply disgraceful. It cannot be said too often—the life of a poor man in this Floating World is essentially worthless.

I sometimes wonder what kind of retribution for deeds in former incarnations divides men into the wealthy and the poor. Rich people have good things come their way without lifting a finger, but poor people can wish and hope, and all they get is one misfortune after another. One can only say that there are times when one simply cannot bear to see or hear of yet another instance of someone's disappointment.

Having good fortune in one's undertakings is by no means limited to members of the merchant class; it can happen among samurai families as well. On the evening of the third day of the first month, as was according to custom, those gentlemen and women who had performed long and loyal service in the household of a certain daimyo were assembled in the front parlor of his mansion to play a game called Reeling Prizes. Stretching from behind the sliding screens separating the parlor from the back rooms were several hundred gaily colored strings. Each person took hold of a string and reeled in whatever was attached to the other end, which he then received as a gift.

A young page reeled in his string only to find, to everyone's amusement, a T-headed mulberry walking-stick just right for some old man; at the end of the string that the daimyo's chief retainer drew in was a bag of coins; someone else pulled in a bolt of Chinese-style silk; and another got a short sword designed for some dignitary, while his neighbor

On the evening of the third day of the first month, as was according to custom, those gentlemen and women who had performed long and loyal service in the household of a certain daimyo were assembled in the front parlor of his mansion to play a game called Reeling Prizes. Stretching from behind the sliding screens separating the parlor from the back rooms were several

hundred gaily colored strings. Each person took hold of a string and reeled in whatever was attached to the other end, which he then received as a gift. . . . Incidentally, among all those people pulling in their rewards one by one, there was not a single person of humble status who reeled in a prize of considerable monetary value.

wound up with an old-fashioned stamping mill for hulling grains.

Others were rewarded with a portable set of nested boxes, a halberd, a seal and inkstone case, a coin purse, a parasol, satin bedding, and an antique ladle. One vassal reeled in some gold coins. The bonze of a certain tea cult became the proud owner of one dried salmon, and equally amusing was the house watchman who, of course, found himself matched with a pair of new spectacles. Incidentally, among all these people pulling in their rewards one by one, there was not a single person of humble status who reeled in a prize of considerable monetary value.

At this point it was the turn of the senior servant of the house, a man eighty-six years old. While being pulled up from his seat by the hand, he wished everyone the best greetings of the season and said that as he was actually a treasure in his own right he would give up his string to let someone else have a chance. When the string was reeled in, one of the parlor maids, Mumegakidono by name, saw a long-sleeved kimono at the other end, one that had been carefully selected in the Capital. "Over here, over here," she selfishly exclaimed, putting a damper on everyone else's fun.

Next it was the turn of the daimyo's political advisor, a young rake known to be fond of the more fleshly pleasures. He took a string from someone else and after saying a few words of prayer reeled in his prize, which turned out to be a one-hundred-and-three-year-old woman called the Old Badger—a holdover from the days of the daimyo's father. At this point one and all joined in a hearty laugh to celebrate the coming of spring. Even the lord of the house was in good spirits, and, as the banquet began with a platter suggestive of the Isle of Eternal Youth, the joyous toast of "Banzai!" filled the air.

• 11 • The arts and what they can do to people

The ancients used to say that when training in the arts you should never get too deeply involved in pursuits outside your own occupation, and I could not agree more.

Chou Yen, a counselor to the King of Yen in China's Warring States period, devoted fifty years to mastering the flute, and in his seventies he achieved an eerie ability with the instrument. Once in the dead heat of the sixth month he played a tune in the wintry mode, and to the delight and astonishment of thousands of witnesses, frost formed over the front garden. It was not long after the attainment of such mastery that Chou Yen passed away from this world. Since he had never seriously considered the consequences of his death, it proved impossible for any of his successors to pick up his mantle, and there was no lasting benefit from this passing amusement.

We also have figures like the Taoist wizard Tso Tz'u and the Japanese sorcerer of the Muromachi period, Kashin Koji, but the practice of their magic was at the root of considerable social upheaval, and their long years of disciplined training profited neither themselves nor the world around them. The first priority for people today should be learning how to read and write in preparation for a life of real scholarship. Nothing else is worthwhile.

Nowadays people's hearts always seem set on the pursuit of things beyond their social means. In times when the race belongs to the fleet-footed, to while away one's days lazing in the shade of a willow tree on the *kemari* playing fields is a perfect example of how to cause oneself nine parts harm without a single redeeming benefit. As long as you carry a lantern and tread softly on dark nights, you won't need *kemari* footwork to keep from falling in the gutter.

Those who practice recreational archery, formerly the exclusive pastime of court ladies, are particularly guilty of putting on airs. Archery somehow seems too tame for a grown man and wholly inappropriate for a workman whose hands are more accustomed to clutching hammers and saws. What does it matter if you score a hundred bull's-eyes, or even one day hang up your shingle as a sharpshooter? On certain occasions, such as shooting a thief, knowing how to use a bow and arrow can at least serve a valid purpose. Or if not this, then perhaps you can shoot your cat if you catch her making off with your fish for supper, but this is not going to impress anyone.

And then we have competitions to see who can distinguish among various kinds of incense. This is the traditional recreation of those elegant men and women of leisure who are blessed with sufficient fortunes to do as they please. But I suppose it is true that a nose trained in the subtleties of different fragrances can actually help to save money by telling you when the rice is burning or when the firewood beneath the kettle should be changed.

Since so much of the tea ceremony hinges on the quality of one's utensils, it is quite beyond the reach of poor people. The tradition is to "trust in the things that you have and value those that are worn." These are the very words of Sen-no-Rikyu, the patriarch of all tea ceremonies, but people from poor families do not find the notion terribly amusing. It would be advisable for people who have well-equipped homes to show their most fashionable things in a restrained way. After all, since we have to live in this world and have dealings with others, we should place ourselves in the middle ranks and learn how to consume the beverage as if we were part of the crowd.

There is also the tradition of Noh-theater orchestration with its challenging Midare-dance accompaniment and even its difficult Dojoji composition. But I have no desire to attain the status of a master, for there is not even any use in becoming an accomplished amateur. It is quite sufficient for one to learn the old favorites so that he can feel at ease at the reception the next time someone from the neighborhood marries.

Performance in amateur shows is best left for one's childhood. When someone with a face sprouting whiskers gets up on the stage and says, "I'd like to introduce myself. I'm . . . ," people fill in the blank with ". . . a big fool." While the restless people in the audience break uneasily into a sweat, only the performer's mother has anything nice to say about him.

The art of flower arrangement was originally the handiwork of priests attached to the imperial court. The priests would take oaks and pines gathered by woodsmen from deep in the mountain forests and arrange them for the amusement of those who lacked the opportunity to see the flowers and blossoms change with the seasons far afield. But these days anyone with a sufficiently brazen spirit will, without hesitation, pluck a grafted camellia or uproot a potted holly. Such people will break off lotus blossoms in sacred precincts, chop down a cryptomeria on a holy mountain, and behave thoroughly willfully. Plants have feelings too, and the sufferings of these flowers must be severe.

All this waste of time and money can be seen in just one day. We see small businessmen with their *go* and chess, samurai with their *shamisen,* merchants with their martial arts, priests with their puppet theaters, and farmers with their books of etiquette, and not one of these does any of them the least bit of good. There are all too many examples of this sort of thing in our society.

Be that as it may, poetry has always been a part of us in this land. Even the bush warbler and the lowly frog raise their voices in verse. Even more so do human beings, whose very humanity is bound up with poetic compositions. Over time the rules for linked-verse composition have relaxed to allow for the emergence of yet another poetical form, which we all call the *haikai.* Formerly *haikai* verses were the pastime of those who had retired from active life in the world, or of the wardens of Shinto shrines, or of the samurai class. Recently, however, *haikai* have grown so popular in our society that every last apprentice and scullery maid tries his or her hand at them.

Generally speaking, though, the arts are such that they degenerate when allowed to fall into the hands of just anyone. In better days *haikai* masters were familiar with the entire corpus of recorded verse, and one learned the correct forms from such knowledgeable people. Nobles and priests received priority in the seating, and in all matters the masters' words were as good as law. Since their hearts were

The art of flower arrangement was originally the handiwork of priests attached to the imperial court. The priests would take oaks and pines gathered by woodsmen from deep in the mountain forests and arrange them for the amusement of those who lacked the opportunity to see the flowers and blossoms change with the seasons far afield.

sincere, their verses automatically conformed to divine intent. Whenever someone in a poetry circle composed a fine link in a chain of verses, the others would gasp with awe and selflessly extol his effort with a single voice. They would transcribe his verse on the ends of their folding fans and show it to friends with similar tastes.

Furthermore, when writing critical commentary on the verses, the markers of that age would take scrolls of one hundred verses and elucidate the texts by transcribing their comments about each individual link onto the margins.* In turn the composers themselves, who understood the principles governing *haikai* poetry, would point out to their markers any errors in the sequence of their verses or any character repetitions that the markers might have overlooked, thus making the drills of mutual benefit.

But look at the persons who pass themselves off as markers today! These same men until yesterday would stun you with the obvious by pointing out such things as, "A horse belongs to the category of living creatures," and if they were asked whether the word "cow" can follow a verse in which the word "darkness" appears, their ignorance would reveal that they have not even learned the first four pages of the *Hanaigusa* book of rules. But today they have gigantic made-to-order seals that leave marks as large as those on bags of sweets, and it is remarkable how many have pen names ending in *-ken*.† They charge one copper for each verse they are supposed to mark, but they skip whole sec-

---

* Thanks to the widespread enthusiasm for *haikai* versification, a master of the form could support himself by teaching the principles of his art to others, and this teaching generally involved the "marking" or grading of a student's verses with critical commentary written in the margins.

† It was a popular practice for artists, men of letters, and, of course, *haikai* markers to affect two-syllable surnames ending in *-ken*.

tions without putting down any commentary and just scribble some general score at the top of the page.

They do not know that if you use the word "dear" in one verse then you cannot use the word "venison" for at least another two verses. They are unaware that mentioning the Arima Spa constitutes a water reference and can never remember whether the kite bird can appear in *haikai* and crows in linked verses or if it is the other way around. In short, they are of no help at all, and since they know as little of things Japanese as some Chinaman, they leave the verses just as they are.

Those markers whose reputations extend throughout the country spent twenty years learning by heart the thousand-and-one rules governing word associations before they reached the level of master, and they always made their pronouncements with perfect judgment no matter what issue was brought to their podiums for deliberation. Those who masquerade as *haikai* masters today should at least take time to attend the class of a real teacher to see how things are done. If one of these charlatans were ever to make a trip to the Sumiyoshi Shrine, the God of Poetry would look past him, and from the inner sanctum would come the words, "A bogus *haikai* master is here." This man, knowing that his prayers would go unanswered, would only be able to hang his head in shame.

When you look at one of our poetry circles, you can see people who put on disagreeable expressions when confronted with a superior piece of work because they can remember a time when *they* presented an inferior verse. The students bypass their teacher and scrutinize their companions' word associations, all the while disregarding the rules. If you think about it carefully, *haikai* masters now seem so foolish because they are crooks.

A *haikai* master who gives an honest judgment of a verse irrespective of the wealth or poverty of its composer is a master worthy of the name. Truly, when it reaches the point where a *haikai* poem is nothing more than the tail end of some other verse, then think what this implies about so-called masters in all the other arts. Perhaps what all this amounts to is that people today have become too clever for their own good.

•12• Second thoughts about passions

Life is like a day of fun. We are born at dawn and in the evening we die. In fact, life is really not much more than a naptime dream. But of all the things that can capture a man's fancy, one thing that has never failed to arouse a man's interest, both in old times and new, at home and abroad, is frolicking with courtesans. Upon hearing a Chinaman strum his lyre and sing of the uninterrupted stream flowing into Feng-ch'iao,* we feel the same erotic sentiments that are prompted by our own country's Nagebushi ballad that is sung in the Shimabara licensed quarters of the Capital. "As long as I'm alive, this love will never die," the words go, and as long as a man has a breath of life left inside him, it is next to impossible for him to change his ways, no matter what his friends or conscience might have to say about it.

Each of us can testify to the countless men in every nook

* Based on the poem, "A Night Spent at Feng-ch'iao," by the T'ang poet Chang Chi.

and cranny of the country who are committed to courtesans and who whittle away at their fortunes until they encounter all manner of hardship. Everyone thinks that this sort of problem will never happen to him, but any man who goes to spend "one day" in play will find himself emptying his pockets and then spending whatever money he is able to scrape up by borrowing. When it reaches the point where he can neither advance nor retreat a single step, he entertains vain hopes of how nice it would be if the rocks in his cart were silver. But he can think what he wants, for he must inevitably grind to a halt and humbly end his cavorting in such places. The men who have reached that point are like samurai without swords, veritable ghosts of their former selves; and it is amusing to observe just how splendidly quiet they can be when utterly bared in this state.

No man has ever managed to live out his days without at least once giving in to the dizzying temptations of courtesans and their lot. If, before it is too late, the gods and Buddhas can only catch a man in the midst of his revelry and get him to put a stop to his gallivanting, then he can at least come out with his house intact, and though his business may have fallen off, he should still be able to maintain his livelihood. As long as he turns himself around and throws himself back into his work, everyone, from the people in his ward down to every last one of his friends and relatives, will pardon his earlier juvenile excesses. It hardly needs repeating, but if there is one area where a man should be discreet it is in the pursuit of carnal pleasures. In ancient times our elders in all their wisdom perceived this truth and bequeathed it to us in their writings.

In those days there lived in the harbor district of Osaka a man of considerable fame who, under the assumption that money is the best tool for gaining more money, carried on the work of his father by running a bank. Never deviating from his single purpose in life, he concentrated on the enterprises with which he was most familiar and eventually grew quite wealthy. He acquired houses and other properties in the better parts of town whose rental income alone amounted to thirty *kamme* a year. He also invested in fields in the Yamato region—always a secure investment—and these earned him an annual yield of four hundred bushels of rice. He bequeathed his treasure of three thousand *kamme* in cash to his eldest son, and passed away leaving behind a one-page testament directing the young man to share the estate with his younger brothers but to give them only enough to prevent their being subjected to ridicule.

Now the heir to this fortune exceeded his parents' intentions, for he was endowed with a disposition even more miserly than that of his father. In the spring of his fifth year, on the occasion of his ceremonial First Wearing of adult clothing, he pressed his trousers himself and put in the creases just the way he wanted them, and when he was saddened because the foil covering on his ball-and-mallet set had peeled off, he rewrapped it in paper and showed it to his father. From then on his father's faith in him was confirmed. Confident of the young man's prospects, he informed the bank's managers that his son would not be the sort ever to fall into dissolute habits.

Time went by, and the son, by age seventeen or eighteen, was rather different from other people. For one thing, he had no contact with those outside his business circles. For another, he lacked any sense of human obligations. Since he preferred the company of complex mathematical calculations and rejoiced only in the opportunity to further the prospects of his family, he spent day and night immersed solely in business matters. His numerous employees, therefore, found it most difficult to ask for days off to go sightseeing or touring in the countryside.

However, people's hearts in this world of ours do sometimes change and can never be taken for granted. By the age of twenty-one the young master had still not discovered the pleasure of a woman's company, and his only amusement in life still seemed to be spending a day in his vaults counting the cash boxes. One day the master heard that a young man whom he employed as a sandal bearer made an occasional practice of emptying his purse by going to the licensed quarters at Shijimi in order to have a bit of sport. The master made inquiries at the tea house in question, and after a thorough survey of the situation he severely admonished the young man and told him on the spot, "You're fired!" whereupon the young man lost all face and dashed home.

Afterward, the proprietor of the tea house called the master aside and said, "Now, what you do is your own affair, but your boy left without paying for his drinks, and I'd like you to take care of the bill." The master was disturbed by this, but when he realized that he could not just pick up and leave without settling the bill, he decided that as long as he was going to pay out good money it would be a sin to return home empty-handed. He then learned for the first time the fascinating things that the hands of a professional woman can teach, and from then on he returned each day for advanced instruction.

One day in the course of his training he encountered an entertainer who suggested that they sample the favors at one of the bathhouses. But when the master saw how degrading the place looked, he redoubled his exertions and began consorting with fifteen-*momme* whores. This seemed especially fine for a time, but his eyes wearied of seeing apprentice courtesans with padded clothing and dirty-collared kimonos. Then he happened to catch sight of the exquisite figure cut by a *tenshoku* courtesan* as she walked down the street, and again his tastes took a more expensive turn. Since he grew increasingly extravagant and gained a considerable reputation as a big spender, not even *tenshoku* were enough, and he began acquainting himself with *tayu*. He showed a gift for this kind of activity, and even the lowliest employees in the houses of assignation rejoiced in the "garari garari" clinking of his coins, which he handed out with a practiced ease as natural as that of a hand moving to scratch an itch. He would strut about hand in hand with a *tayu* and had no qualms over spending whatever it took to insure his priority over other callers; even if they had had a lover's quarrel, he was always her favorite customer.

"They say the world's a big place," he boasted, "but in case someone would like to see who's the best spender, just let him step forward and we'll give it a go. Even if it should take a hundred years, you can bet I'm man enough to spend what it takes. I'm one customer in this world with enough to spare, and you know why? I'm young, healthy, and have plenty of money; my father is dead and I know how to use my wits. I'm generous, deeply compassionate, and I don't drink, so with the whole year to do as I please, there isn't a thing I lack.

"I pay the girls' fees in advance. They can come and go as they please whenever they want. I give the madam as much pocket money for the girls as they ask for. Other *tayu* worry when they haven't booked any New Year's customers by the twenty-fourth or -fifth day of the twelfth month, and may even resort to sending solicitous letters to utterly unacceptable men. To read one of these letters is

---

* A courtesan of the second rank, below a *tayu*.

"Now, what you do is your own affair, but your boy left without paying for his drinks, and I'd like you to take care of the bill." The master was disturbed by this, but when he realized that he could not just pick up and leave without settling the bill, he decided that as long as he was going to pay out good money it would be a sin to return home empty-handed. He then learned

for the first time the fascinating things that the hands of a professional woman can teach, and from then on he returned each day for advanced instruction. . . . For fourteen or fifteen years, people looked on until he had not a hundred coppers left to his name.

enough to bring tears to your eyes. But none of my girls need ever suffer that kind of humiliation. They just leave everything to me, and as long as I'm not too busy, I'll send any order they give me in the winter to Kyoto, where, according to their specifications, they can have cotton *yukata* dyed in time for the Festival of All Souls or specially designed kimonos for the Chrysanthemum Festival.

"It's a wonderful thing how, for a customer as reliable as this, the girls will get up when they're sleepy or will look so sad when I have to leave. The madams carefully check the sakè, and if they let me drink it you can be sure there's nothing wrong with it. The proprietors also pay attention to detail, so they'll never serve me grilled herring in the winter, since herring appear in the autumn and by wintertime have lost their novelty.

"I'm not your ordinary customer who has to have things measured out for him. There are people obviously on the verge of bankruptcy who ask the proprietor to arrange for a girl on one of the holidays when prices are higher. Should the proprietor curb this senseless waste, they will turn instead to eating and drinking their fill and then leave after running up a huge bill. People like this should not be mentioned in the same breath with me.

"Likewise, it's an uncomfortable situation when the girls receive holiday money that comes from a man who has mortgaged his house or borrowed. Just have them come and coax the money out of me. I'll wager I'm the only fun-loving man in this part of town who will back down from no man, because I can always pay one thousand *kamme* in my favorite house."

All this he said in his most conceited way. But money can often be a man's worst enemy, and while everyone listened to his boasts as though they made perfect sense, they knew that when a man becomes too extravagant in his ways he will not be around much longer. For fourteen or fifteen years, people looked on until he had not a hundred coppers left to his name—this is how remarkably he squandered his money.

Formerly he had always been the one to poke fun at others, but now he was the one to lurk in the shadows of the Nagamachi slum, making fireworks and incense sticks and never knowing if he would make it from morning to nightfall. He had his widowed mother train herself to spin cotton and sold his younger sister into service at a house of ill repute. When the advance from her sale arrived, he gleefully stole away to engage in more of his madness with the streetwalkers.

One night in the eleventh month, after the outdoor fair season had passed, he picked up a whore named Tiger Lady in the Yoshiwara district. In the flickering light of a *hibachi* brazier, she recognized him. But he did not mind, and joked with her. "In better times I was a man who could afford fresh underclothing every day, but now I would not even be ashamed to wear Katsuma undies. People really are funny, but don't you go making fun of me."

From this one error in judgment—always buying women—he wound up like this. He is by no means the only one.

•13• The traveling salesman who sold advice

At the bottom of the ocean there is a hole called Wei-lu.*
Day after day and night after night, the rivers of the world
empty their waters into the sea, but thanks to the fact that
surplus water has a chance to drain out of this hole, there
is no rise in the water level. Likewise, human beings have
an opening that resembles the Wei-lu hole. In his lifetime
a man puts an infinite amount of food into his mouth morning, noon, and night. . . .

Now, there are a thousand and one ways of making a
living, but whichever of these occupations a man steps into,
he should never be careless. As long as a man sticks to the
straight and true and works himself to the bone, he is acting
in accordance with divine providence, and there is no way
that he can fail in his livelihood.

Generally speaking, since people are always flocking to
provincial castle towns and harbors there should be any

* The story of the Wei-lu hole is in the "Autumn Waters" chapter of the *Chuang Tzu*.

number of ways for a man to make a living in those places. However, look at the town of Fushimi in Yamashiro Province and try to imagine how it was seventy or eighty years ago. A hint of the onetime prosperity of the houses along both sides of the grand boulevards still shines through, but over the years the place has grown more and more desolate, and now there are countless souls living there who, without any notion of how to do business, let the months and years slip by. When you think about it, it suggests the saying, "In a town of a thousand rooftops, we all pull along together."

In recent years people have become ever so crafty, and it is nearly impossible to make a decent living if you do ordinary kinds of work. Last year in the twelfth month there were men who made the rounds replastering furnaces, and one might think that they had found a fine niche for themselves, but at this year's end even handier men went about offering to polish pots and pans. They charged five *mon* for a large pot and two *mon* for anything smaller.

There are also men who wash other people's rice. They charge four *mon* per bushel for this service, which is of great use to families short of hands. Similarly, there was a man whose appearance suggested that he was a craftsman moonlighting from a housewares store. He went about carrying rulers, bamboo spatulas, paint brushes, and glue from door to door and charged one *mon* to wallpaper a six-foot section of living room wall, two *mon* to repaper a sliding door, and one *mon* for any lantern, and he even swept up after himself. Whenever someone bought a guardian figurine, this man would come over armed with hooks and nails, determine the most auspicious place to hang it, and go home. It certainly is an age full of opportunity for the right person. These are all household services, but they are definitely not intended for your below-average man.

There was also a fiftyish-looking man who would hang a knapsack from his shoulder and make the rounds while calling out, "Let me take the fleas off your cats!" Old retired people who cherished their calico cats would stop him and say, "Here, take it." Having fixed his price at three *mon* per cat, this man would then perform his service in a most remarkable fashion. First he would pour warm water on the cat and wash it, and then, while it was still wet, he would wrap it in a wolf skin. While the cat was snuggled up like this, the fleas would find the wetness of its fur so uncomfortable that they would all jump over to the wolf skin, which the man would then shake out onto the roadway. I don't know how he ever struck upon an idea like this, but it was one way for him to make a living.

Nowadays most people are clever, and in this world of ours where people understand one another without having to exchange a word there lived a gentleman of respectable age who looked like a man of the world, for he carried a short sword at his side and a large purse slung from his belt. He made the rounds wearing a leather overcoat and would haughtily call out, "If something is troubling you, just come call on me no matter what it might be! Personal finances are my specialty so let's talk it over and sort it all out!"

Anyone with sense in his head would never listen to this. But your average man in the street, all the while thinking, "What kind of bastard child of the God of Swindlers do we have here?" would nevertheless gasp with astonishment and crane his neck to get a better look.

In the autumn of last year some men hired a boat by the mouth of the Sangen'ya River to take them goby fishing. After getting rowdy from all the sakè, they barbecued the gobies they had caught and had a contest to see who could eat the most of them. In the middle of their gluttonous

In the middle of their gluttonous game, one of them took a fish and tried to swallow it whole, but immediately his throat began to hurt. When his friends looked to find out what was wrong, they saw that hanging from the fish's stomach was a two-inch piece of fishing line whose hook, still attached, had gotten caught in their friend's throat.

game, one of them took a fish and tried to swallow it whole, but immediately his throat began to hurt. When his friends looked to find out what was wrong, they saw that hanging from the fish's stomach was a two-inch piece of fishing line whose hook, still attached, had gotten caught in their friend's throat. No matter what they did, the hook would not budge, and there seemed no way to help their friend out of his misery. With the boat's drum and *shamisen* silenced, they felt as helpless as the priest whose head got stuck in the pot in Yoshida Kenko's *Tsurezuregusa*.*

With their friend's life now in danger, they rushed him home and showed him to a doctor, who found himself equally at a loss. The respectable-looking swindler whom I mentioned earlier came passing by just as they were conferring on what to try next, and when they told him what had happened, he said, "I'll have that hook out in a minute." He took some small beads off a rosary and strung them one by one onto the line leading to the hook that was caught in the man's throat. Then he gently pulled the string taut, and by working it up a little at a time, he managed to remove the hook without the least bit of difficulty. To a man, all were amazed at his incredible ingenuity.

Among those who witnessed this performance was a man who could never bear not having his own say. "I have a bit of a request too, sir," he chimed in. "Recently everything has been going wrong for my business, and whether I try to do something about it myself or whether I try to let things sort themselves out, my losses just keep piling up. What's more, these difficulties of mine are common knowledge, and no one will extend my credit, so I'm increasingly hard pressed. And what with the holidays coming up, no matter

* In Chapter 53 of that work.

how I figure it when I check my accounts, I still find myself more than twenty *kamme* short. I'd really appreciate the benefit of your counsel."

"Does your wife come from a rich family," asked the miracle worker, "or do you have any younger brothers who happen to be wealthy priests?"

"I'm afraid the answer's no on both counts," replied the man.

"Then I'm afraid I can't help you." And with those words he picked himself up and went home.

• 14 • The bridge of the landlady's nose

Whether you happen to be a businessman or an artisan, never move from a place that you are accustomed to. The common folk have a saying: "Even a stone will warm up if you sit on it for three years." There is nothing quite as painful to observe as people packing up their belongings while the pots on the stove are still warm.

Generally speaking, similar things group themselves together, and business shops are no exception. Even people in the provinces are aware that sharkskin shops, herbal medicine stores, and bookstalls can all be found on Second Avenue. And anyone who wears a hat, whether he be a Kagura performer at the Ise Shrine or one of the hawkers of lucky amulets at the Kashima Shrine, knows that there have long been haberdashers along Karasuma Avenue. Whenever occasion demands a hat, even if only to cheer a hearty "Banzai!" or to do a lucky dance, people go there to be outfitted in whatever they require. The owners of these shops can, without actively hawking their wares, sit at home and be assured of a steady stream of business.

Along Seventh Avenue in the downtown part of the Capital lived a man in a small rented home who made a business out of manufacturing folding fans in the spring and summer and tailoring hand-scrubbed paper kimonos from the end of autumn on through the winter. Pilgrims journeying to the Hongan temples would often stop and order something from the shop as a souvenir, and the financial prospects of the store grew considerably until for once there was a bit of money around.

One day while chatting over a cup of tea with her friends from the neighborhood, the fan maker's wife laughingly said, "You know, our landlady has the most extraordinary nose. It looks like they used it as bait for the demon at Mount Atago."

Near their table happened to be a flattering sycophant of a woman. When she told the landlady of what had been said, the landlady burst out, "I inherited this nose from my parents and had nothing to do with it. But I'll defer to the wishes of the wives of my tenants and have my face changed so you won't find it so hard to look at. But I'm not about to make the bridge of my nose into a piece of merchandise like some harlot. My husband vowed to put up with this nose for the rest of his life and he's managed to bear it quite handsomely for the past nineteen years, so I never thought that anything else was all that important. Why, I never realized how difficult I was making life for all of you! In any case I'll have the situation fixed before the day is through."

Since what she had said made so little sense, the ladies became quite upset and said, "Even if it were only for one day, we live under your roof and so you get the same respect as our own husbands. If *she* says that your mouth is large, that's just *her* flapping tongue. Or about your flat feet—*she's* been going on and on for days about how if you

had your dresses cut extra long, no one would ever notice."
In this way they all laid the blame on the fan maker's wife.

The landlady grew even more enraged and said, "Well, well, Mrs. Fan Maker, so you think my nose is too long? I've noticed that the eaves of your house obstruct the walkway and make it hard for people to come and go, so you'd just better vacate the premises—immediately!"

The fan maker's wife laughed sarcastically and said, "Well, well, madam, the Capital is a big place and as long as we pay our rent each month, I'm sure we'll have no trouble finding a house where the roof doesn't leak and the people have normal noses."

"Well, well, my dear. For your information, among the ranks of those with long noses, there once was a princess named Suetsumu, but since common folk like you never look at *The Tale of Genji*, we can't expect you to know that sort of thing."

"My mother, I'll have you know, was a lady in the Imperial Palace, and I've even ridden in the royal carriage."

"Well, well, since people who aren't really accustomed to riding in carriages find it difficult, you'd be safer to ride in one of those coffins made by your father—the cooper!"

"Oh really? Did we ask our dear friend to inquire into our ancestry? But since you've brought it up, you've always said that you were the only child of the chief warden at the Izumo Shrine; but then why did you marry into such humble quarters? Why, I would think the gods would be most displeased that in all of Japan you couldn't find a more appropriate match. Surely there must be someone in this world who could better meet your standards. At the Fudeya tavern in Saga there used to be a long-nosed siren named Koman, and none of us is unaware of her resemblance to a certain landlady. I've even heard that she's living somewhere right here in the Capital!" And on and on she went in a similar vein.

The landlady flushed with rage. "Just get out of this house and we'll have nothing further to argue about!" she yelled, and she unlatched the door and went home.

When he heard about what had happened, the fan maker was enraged with his wife and said, "Our having to abandon this place that we're used to, all because of your mouth, will be the death of our livelihood. I want you to apologize to the landlady."

But his wife changed her expression and said, "That's out of the question."

"To go against a man's order is grounds for divorce. Get out of here while you still have the skin on your back!"

"Then I guess I'd better go. But if you're really going to throw me out, I think I'll let everyone know just what the real circumstances were at the time of your older sister's rather sudden death. Well, I think I'll go now." And with these words she started packing.

But her husband pressed his hands together and reconsidered. "Oh, it's bad enough to have to move, but do we have to add a divorce on top of it? Deep down inside I also found it hard to put up with that landlord's wife and all her haughtiness. I suppose we'll just have to move." And so they did, to Samegai ward on Fifth Avenue. Their new neighbor on the southern side was a woman who for some years had been quite deranged and who would without the slightest warning pull out a cleaver and terrorize the neighborhood by wandering about hacking at things. They left this place as well and moved to a house in front of the Rokkakudo Temple.

People said that the house had been built long ago with the main pillar put in upside down, and each evening the

They . . . moved to a house in front of the Rokkakudo Temple. People said that the house had been built long ago with the main pillar put in upside down, and each evening the curved beams would creak and moan so loudly that the couple would awaken, afraid that the house was coming down around them.

SOME FINAL WORDS OF ADVICE

(Note: These two illustrations describe a composite image of the horrors faced by the hapless couple. The inversion of household furnishings on the right and the inversion of the entire scene on the left are visual allusions to the upside-down main pillar, which had the effect of turning their world "topsy-turvy.")

curved beams would creak and moan so loudly that the couple would awaken, afraid that the house was coming down around them. They left this place, too, and switched over to Sembon Avenue.

Here they were delighted to find a quiet little home, but each time there was a westerly wind, smoke from the nearby crematorium would waft in and bring out all the insects as well. Since neither the fan maker nor his wife was particularly fond of the little bugs, they found this place an awful bother and again decided that it was time for a change. This time they moved to Shincho Street just north of Fourth Avenue, where they found a small but newly built one-family house.

Their neighbor on the north was the retired proprietor of a lacquerware shop whose house had a lovely latticed front and who minded his own business. On the southern side were liquor and malt stores as well as the magnificent houses of many prominent people. "Now we've finally found just what we've been looking for," they thought to themselves, thoroughly pleased. But from that first evening on they couldn't even hear each other speak, for their pillows echoed all night long with the sound of Buddhist chanting emanating from the house of that nice retired gentleman who just happened to belong to the Senshu sect of the Pure Land church. What's more, thousands of cockroaches as big as cicadas swarmed in from the malt store next door. They gnawed their way into the tableware box, jumped into the water for tea, chewed up clothing, made holes in the rice bags, made a shambles of the folding screens, ruined strings of dried fish, worked their way into bottles of soy sauce, left their droppings in the salt box, and did who knows what other damage.

If the ancients had only known about such things, they

would probably have written, "A roach in the house means drunks throughout the land."* In any case, the couple found it impossible to spend the summer in this house and soon retreated to new quarters.

In the space of two years they moved no less than nine times, and what little savings they had soon dwindled to almost nothing. They then moved to the vicinity of the Niitama Tsushima Shrine on Matsubara Avenue at the prompting of the wife's younger half-brother, who also lived there. Now this house happened to be northeast of their old house, and when the fan maker noticed this he remarked, "Why, this even corresponds to where the Metals Spirit is dwelling this year!"†

But his brother-in-law scoffed at this and said, "In this day and age who has the time to pay attention to curses? Just leave everything to me." Thus ignoring common sense, he moved them into the house. But nothing at all went their way, and day and night their fortunes waned until their livelihood was as disheveled as the forty-eight layers of a paper kimono.

Finally the couple decided to part and make their ways separately. The husband moved to a place called Shiraichi in Mutsu Province, where he worked as an apprentice in a paper-clothing store, and his wife moved to the island of Hirado, where she made her living making folding fans.

* An allusion to Chapter 97 of *Tsurezuregusa*.
† The direction northeast was believed to be the most unlucky, since it was the direction from which evil spirits would enter. Thus, any move to the northeast of one's former abode was thought ill-fated. The Metals Spirit lived in a different direction each year, with eight years forming a complete cycle. Any move in the direction of the Metals Spirit was similarly thought to be unlucky, and in this instance the two compounded each other. These notions were imported from China, where they formed part of the *yin-yang* cosmology, but they were taken no less seriously in Japan.

Their being forced to live at different ends of the country like this was all because of the needless excesses of this woman's mouth. In general, if there is one thing about which a woman should be especially prudent, it is her speech. At the time when they were about to take leave of each other, they lamented their decision, and with the sleeves of their robes washed with tears, they said to each other, "Oh, when will our paths cross again? Goodbye, goodbye."

But the wife had a change of heart and thought that no matter what she might have promised this man there was no sense in a married couple's living hundreds of miles apart. So she firmly told her husband that she would have divorce papers drawn up and bring the matter to a close.

After hearing this, the husband began to quarrel severely with her and said, "How do you expect to make a living all by yourself?"

But his wife screamed back at him as she drew away. "And you're so sure you can live without a woman? You filthy thief of your elder sister's money!"

How true it is that when two people divorce they might as well be perfect strangers. And how frightening people's hearts can be.

•15• A bill collector's life...and death

I once inquired into why the term "*ema* doctors" is used to refer to physicians whose practices are less than flourishing.

Once upon a time there was a doctor who, having no carriage of his own, made his house calls on foot. He wished to leave the countryside and set up residence in Osaka, and finally, in the midst of his financial troubles, he took what little savings he had, left his wife behind, and rented a little house there. He built a bamboo wicker fence around it, and on the post of the main gate he hung a sign with his name painted on it in large, bold letters.

Thinking that he could perform his singular miracles in the event of any emergency in the neighborhood, he awaited his opportunity day and night. But not a single soul came to avail himself of his services, and there seemed to be little he could do about it. Just sitting at home came to be impossible, and he began to spend his days touring shrines and temples in Osaka.

One time when he was invited to join in some late-night chatter with the men on neighborhood patrol, one gentleman remarked, "You see that fierce wind out there tonight? That's because it's the first of the eleventh month; the gods are returning home all over the country.* How frightening the sky is! Doesn't that dark cloud look just like a goblin?"

This prompted one of the other men to say, "What about that *ema* painting† of Omori Hikoshichi given to the Temma Tenjin Shrine? That Yamamoto Mon'emon could paint! What a masterpiece!"

But when the man finished speaking, our doctor friend put on a sullen expression and said, "I think you may all have overlooked something about that painting. There's a mistake in the portrayal of Hikoshichi. He forgot to paint in the cord on his court hat."

Everyone clapped in astonishment and said, "What an incredible eye for detail you have!"

But this was not the end of the story, for sometime thereafter our "knowledgeable" doctor was invited to the home of a prominent physician who informed him, "Even artists had to have a thorough knowledge of their subjects. Centuries ago in Hikoshichi's time, people used to hide the cords of their hats by tucking them in with their hair. People did not start tying the cords under their chins until only some hundred years ago!"

When he finished his talk, everyone again clapped in astonishment and said, "Well, well, now."

Generally speaking, since *ema* paintings are noticed by

---

* The tenth month was known as the "godless month" since it was during this period that all local gods gathered at Izumo for their annual conference.

† *Ema* are paintings given as votive offerings to shrines and temples.

"What about that ema painting of Omori Hikoshichi given to the Temma Tenjin Shrine? That Yamamoto Mon'emon could paint! What a masterpiece!" But when the man finished speaking, our doctor friend put on a sullen expression and said, "I think you may all have overlooked something about that painting. . . ."

so many people, they can become quite important. In most cases their importance is only short-lived, but this is not always true. For example, in the Kiyomizu Temple in the Capital hangs an *ema* painting by Hasegawa Nagakura that shows the famous battle between Soga Goro and Asaina Yoshihide. Just above the fold on the inner thigh of Asaina's trousers, Nagakura carelessly drew in a crest of the Dancing Crane pattern. This mistake, when discovered by a servant girl in a dyer's shop on Inokuma Avenue, became the absolute talk of the Capital, and it haunted Nagakura for the rest of his life.

There is also the story about the *ema* painting by Bessho Gon'emon that hangs in the Gion Shrine. The painting depicts a dark and stormy night; Taira Tadanori is grappling with a giant who, bearing a sacred taper and wearing a straw hat, was taken for a demon by the local people. If you imagine putting back together the pieces of clay from the bucket that the giant dropped during the fracas, you would have enough for four or five plates—a fact first discovered by an artisan who sold clay bell-souvenirs in front of the Fushimi Inari Shrine.

When this discovery became common knowledge, informed people had much to say about it. "This is quite a different instance of observation from the case of the Dancing Crane crest. Perhaps the taper-bearing giant actually had five clay plates with him. Unfortunately, we don't have the man around today to ask what really happened," they joked, and the matter was left at that.

Now the doctor of whom I was speaking earlier was still finding it hard to come up with any patients whom he could examine in detail. Since he had nothing to keep himself busy through the year, he occupied himself with rather useless pursuits. For example, he made such startling observations as that the statue of King Emma, the Guardian of Hades, which stood at the Gappo crossroads, had sloping shoulders instead of square ones, or that in one of the wards in Dojima there were handsome young men who looked like the brothers of courtiers. He found it quite impossible, however, to make a name for himself in the field of medicine. Though he of course could have stooped to making hand copies of his many medical books, these texts remained quite untouched, despite all the free time he had.

While the benevolence of a doctor is akin to that of a sage, it is much too roundabout a path for a doctor to assume that people will automatically come calling for him in this world. Unless he makes an effort, people will pass him by.

The famous Irenokoshi eye-medicine store had its humble origins long ago and used the following stratagem to become what it is today. Whenever off-season summer clams were down to three *mon* per half-gallon, the proprietor would buy one half-gallon of clams each day and distribute them free to people in the neighborhood. "You take the flesh and I'll take the shell," he would say, and people then would think, "My, but his eye medicine must be selling well!" His reputation grew in the neighborhood and then spread far and wide throughout the country. Finally he became quite a wealthy man, and he now has any number of branch stores.

Another story concerns a certain doctor who at New Year's would prepare an ointment with not the least bit of medical value. To this he gave the grandiose name Sterling Virtue, and on the bottle he wrote the promise "Good for all ailments." Donning a borrowed medical-looking smock, he would set out before dawn on the day after New Year's and distribute the salve free of charge. It goes without saying that he covered all the houses in his neighborhood. But he also managed to give some to people who were chatting while waiting for boats at the Fushimi docks, to parishioners whom he encountered on their way to temples, to theatergoers whose boxes he shared, and even to people he met in the public bathhouses. In short, he was able to distribute his ointment to just about everyone with whom he came into contact.

He regarded these New Year's gifts as if they were the "seed money" a businessman pays to trade with China, and he continued his exertions for two or three years. The beneficiaries of his presents at first felt a bit sorry for his apparent madness, but he stayed in their minds, and whenever there was something like one of their servants coming down with a cold they would call on his services. Before you knew it he became rather prominent. Looking at it as a part of any good samurai's stock in trade, he had a tailor make him a light blue crepe long coat. Wearing this he ostentatiously traveled about with both a sandal bearer and a personal servant. This gave people confidence in him.

He took the daughter of a masterless samurai as his wife, a girl whose marriage prospects had been bleak but who came with a meager dowry that nevertheless enabled him to afford a small palanquin carried by two men, one of them a regular servant in his household and the other a man hired part-time just for this purpose. Although the whole picture was a bit unseemly—his bearers were of uneven heights and they often had to take breathers while resting on their staffs—when he first set out riding high up there, people drank in the exquisite appearance of their physician in his palanquin and gladly paid five *mon* for a bottle of elixir that had cost two *mon* to produce, thanking him profusely to boot.

If he had thought of the significance of these actions, he would have said a prayer to Shen Nung.* For if he were to have resumed his former practice of making his rounds on foot, he would have found himself in the difficult position of having to explain that he no longer rode in the palanquin because it was impossible to make a proper examination when one was up so high. Once a doctor rides in a palanquin, he had better plan on doing so permanently.

If a doctor makes house calls on foot, he can always laze away his slow days by looking at *ema* paintings, but if he sets out in a palanquin and has no particular place to go, then he is really in trouble and will wind up wasting his day watching an archery competition at someone's mansion or getting into some lengthy discussion over Ishida Mitsumori's role in the Battle of Sekigahara or aimlessly drinking tea at a place where everyone is in all too good health.

If one looks at actual social conditions, however, every four or five years without fail an epidemic occurs. At such times an experienced physician can reap the benefits of his skillful ministering to the sick. If exceptionally good luck comes his way, his reputation will spread, and one day he may even have a spare palanquin bearer!

Truly the bane of every physician's life is a patient who grows impatient with his progress and goes off to some other doctor. But there are also times when new patients come to a doctor, so he should regard the process as something that evens out in the long run. Another occasion that grates on a doctor's nerves and makes him gray before his time is when, having prescribed some medicine for a patient in the evening, he examines him the next morning and is told, "That medicine you told me to take yesterday upset my

---

* A Chinese god-sage revered as the founder of the healing arts.

stomach and I felt dizzy and got cold feet and couldn't speak." Or he may call on a patient whose mother will shriek while tears pour down her cheeks, "The diarrhea just wouldn't stop and he has an awful fever, and he's been babbling 'I want to eat with the Buddha, let me go, let me go,' and we didn't know if he would make it through the night."

Sometimes he will make a house call on a patient who complains, "My chest hurts and my whole mouth is swollen and I can't even roll over in my sleep. Why, I had no idea a man could get this weak so quickly!"

As if this were not sad enough, there are times when a patient's relatives will be gathered in the kitchen and the doctor will have to tell them, "At this point medicine would only kill the patient. I told you from the start that there was no use in calling in a doctor, but you thought you knew better, and all I can advise is that you send someone to the temple to summon a priest." Words like these cut to the quick, and the doctor, wondering just what kind of karma dictated that he be born to such a profession, just wants to run out of the room. They say there are a thousand and one ways for a man to make a living, but being a doctor should surely be at the bottom of the heap. It is especially trying on a doctor's soul when he takes on a difficult case and knows the best he can do is make an educated guess.

Now in this metropolis of Osaka there is no shortage of patients with strange and exotic diseases, but no matter into whose hands they fall, an incurable disease is an incurable disease. On the islet of Nakanoshima there is a seventeen-year-old girl, an only child, who is beautiful in every respect except for having been born with gray hair. It is a terrible pity. Or in Tamazukuri there is a sixteen-year-old girl who has not moved her bowels in four years though her diet is perfectly normal. Then there is the nineteen-year-old girl in Nagahori who on her first birthday pulled herself up to a standing position and since that day has been unable to sleep lying down for one moment. All year long she spends her days just pacing back and forth at home.

Can there be records of cases like these even in Chinese medical books? Since these girls all belong to wealthy families, their parents can afford to hide their embarrassment and still grieve. You could get five hundred *chokin* for curing any one of them, but the cases are all hopeless. Ah, would that the healing Buddha, Yakushi, could appear in a dream and give us an elixir to help these poor unfortunates!

But, you know, there is nothing that varies as much in price as doctors' fees. One doctor prescribes eighty pills and takes five *momme* for them, but another will give you three pills and expect casks of sakè and presents of boxed fish on top of the five *chokin* he charged you! People say that there are three kinds of friends to treasure in the world—rich men, wise men, and doctors. But of these three, never live in a town without a doctor, for it is to him that you entrust your one and only life.

One thing true for all people is that there is no point in living unless you have your health. Make it a rule to give up moxa cautery, to cut out abalone broth and heavy drinking, and to exercise your body while resting your spirit. Your health is the one thing that truly matters.

They say it is a fact of human relations that nothing tests a long-standing friendship like an illness. Since, when you were ill, your illness was a drain on your friends' resources, at first you are conscientious about calling at all hours to inquire about the condition of a friend when he is sick. But even though you had relied upon him in your own time of need, as his infirmity extends for month after month it becomes bothersome to visit, and sooner or later your true nature is put to the test. Even the bond between parent and child will be strained if one is called to nurse the other, for the store of mutual affection will run its course and all the worst instincts will come to the surface.

For a woman there is nothing that compares in urgency to the time when the man on whom she completely relies is taken ill. If his condition is critical, she will resolve to follow him in death. Over time, however, her resolve weakens, and before he has breathed his last she will consider the prospects of his death. "The next man I marry will be different. It makes me sick the way this one's become so disgustingly weak." She will make an inventory of all the articles in the house, including her husband's, and before long, as she awaits her new life, she will become careless about fetching warm water to ease his fever.

But a man, too, finding it tedious when his wife suffers a lengthy illness, will hope that his wait for the final moment will be shortened, if only by a single day. If by some chance he is not careless when looking after his ill wife, it is only because of his hopes concerning the will. Since we live in a world where greed is the dominating principle even among parents and their children, it is always a good idea to make certain that you leave some money behind. This is what is called "Death's silver lining."

Of all the ways in which death can separate people, it is sadder to lose a wife than a parent, but it is the most heartrending of all to lose a child. When you lose your first child it is enough to destroy all desire to carry on in this world, but after you have lost two or three children, your heart becomes devilishly cold and your mourning becomes increasingly transparent. You lose all sympathy for the sufferings of others, and your only thoughts are of yoking your carriage to depart through the gates of this flaming house of a world.

But the most painful thing of all in the world is to watch a suffering child. This is something you cannot understand unless you have children of your own. A certain man did not have his first son until the blessed event occurred quite unexpectedly when he was well into his fifties, and what is more the son was truly one in a hundred. Those who saw the child all remarked that such a precious child could not belong to so humble a family. Since by the age of three the lad could already write in large characters the words for "flower," "bird," "wind," and "moon" without any training, his doting parents called him a reincarnation of Kobo Daishi.*

But in the spring of that year, the child came down with intestinal parasites, and even though every conceivable medicine was administered to him there was no sign of improvement. Just when he lay with half-closed and darkening eyes—showing that he had reached his final moments—and there was weeping all around him, the grocery store where the family's account had been piling up over the year sent a messenger who relentlessly announced, "Pay up the money you owe us!"

The father of the lad thrust out his chest in fury and sent him off saying, "What do you mean by coming in here?"

But the messenger came again. "We never agreed that you needn't pay your bills if the boy should die!" he said, and in the middle of all this shouting, the child passed away. Then, as the room filled with tears and piteous cries, the father stabbed this character from the grocery store, and then killed himself as well.

* The famous ninth-century priest-calligrapher.

• 16 • Ise—where they know you at a glance

Surely there is no shrine as dear to us as the holy Ise Shrine. From all over the country pilgrims come traveling tens of thousands of leagues over mountains and waters, for once a person, rich or poor, man or woman, has been possessed by the desire to visit this shrine, he or she will eventually bring that wish to fruition.

Especially in the spring, the pilgrims are like a mountain on the march, their packhorses bedecked in flowers and drawn in endless lines alongside them. Field trips arrive from every village and hamlet, with two or three hundred pilgrims from one of these villages alone, and since they are all placed in the charge of a single priest, pilgrims from east and west and a dozen different provinces mingle together in delightful confusion. But no matter which of the several priests these pilgrims are charged to, each of the fifteen hundred to three thousand worshipers receives equal treatment.

The kitchen facilities that feed so many people are a marvel of ingenuity. All the necessary utensils are carefully set at both the head table and the number two table. Although one might suspect that unless there were two hundred hired hands working in the kitchen the task of feeding two or three thousand people would be well nigh an impossibility, the entire task is performed by a mere twenty men. First, bowls and chopsticks are placed on individual trays and then plates and other utensils are arranged alongside, all of this being done by three men. Instead of having to wait for the water to heat, the men place the rice in screen baskets that they then lower into the boiling water. The fish that go into the broth are not cleaned and sliced on carving boards but are sliced directly over the large vats to avoid wasting time in the carving.

Of all dishes, the preparation of fish salad is particularly vexatious, so old men are hired. These men don work trousers, and with thin knives in each hand they cut and wrap the ingredients in pieces of cheesecloth. The men are paid for their work at the rate of two *fun* per five gallons. Each can slice fifty gallons a day, and their skill and speed are so remarkable that their output probably could not be equalled by fifteen ordinary cooks. As for the salad dressing, all its ingredients are dumped into a large, shallow tub and are sloshed around with a garden hoe in full view of everyone.

This is the way things should be, but it is the ability to prepare any variety of grilled fish, or rather the ability to place piping hot fish before two thousand guests, that strikes me as being particularly remarkable. One might suppose that they have some fifty *hibachi* or that a hundred-foot ditch where the fish can be grilled is dug in the backyard. The entire chore, however, is performed by just three men humming nonchalantly.

Taking just ten utensils like trowels used to plaster a wall, the men heat them on a *hibachi* until they are red hot. Then twenty fish at a time are put into square baskets that in turn are lowered into a caldron of boiling water. After parboiling, the fish are arranged on long planks, where just one side is rapidly scorched with a hot trowel. The fish are then served with the scorched side up. This Ise barbecue, mind you, is no half-baked affair; the array of culinary techniques is truly most extraordinary.

Thanks to the shrine, the area around Ise offers people a wide range of opportunities for making a living throughout the year. People like masterless samurai and doctors with time on their hands are paid to write letters to the provinces soliciting donations of the first fruits from each harvest. They receive one *momme* eight *fun* per sheaf of high-grade Sugihara paper and one *momme* three *fun* per sheaf dashed off on middle-grade Sugihara paper.

Of course, businessmen in the area, not to mention functionaries of the shrine, are all very clever people who conceal this shrewder side of the Ise operation from visitors. No one knows who started the practice, or when, but another example of this Ise shrewdness is the Pigeon's Eye strings of lead coins. Each is sold as a string of one hundred coins, but each actually has only sixty. For every *kammon* you buy, then, you wind up with one *momme* and four or five *fun* worth of coins to use as offerings on your shrine tours.

The pilgrims on tour start with the Rain Shrine and end up at the Wind Shrine, chattering away to one another with things like: "And here we have the shrine to the God of Marriage. You know, this is where girls come to pray for smooth childbirths without a midwife" or "This is the god who helps girls with their mothers-in-law." If they catch sight of a young man making the tour, they explain his appearance and expression by saying, "Oh yes, do you see which shrine he's visiting? That's the one where young men go when they've been disinherited to pray for their parents' forgiveness."

The priests affiliated with the main shrine may each be responsible for as many as five or six of the branch shrines, and they greedily request donations, saying, "The *mon* you give us will bring you a thousand *kamme*. Be generous when you throw your offerings!" Most people prefer to throw Pigeon's Eye coins into the coffers, and it would be hard to say just how much loss each year is suffered by pilgrims throughout Ise on this account. In fact, just recently the use of the Pigeon's Eye coins was officially prohibited.

Another amusing feature of Ise life is the beggar girls at Ainoyama, a little mound between the Inner and Outer shrines. In former times they dressed in colorful short-sleeved kimonos as courtesans did, but now they hold out bean-curd strainers into which they coax people to toss money. The picture is rather unseemly.

Two of these girls, Otama and Osugi by name, were both beauties who attended to their looks and who strummed their *shamisen* singing, " . . . how sad is the fate of a woman," and other Ise ballads. Every day pilgrims would stop, momentarily enchanted by the pair, and try to hit the girls in the face with coins thrown through the holes in a crimson netting strung before them. But for years not a single coin ever found its mark, for the girls had acquired considerable skill in effortlessly dodging the projectiles.

Then one day a man came from Edo to visit the shrine, and of the hundred coins which he threw, one found its way to Otama's face, where it left an insignificant scar on her forehead. Thereafter eager people came in droves from all over the country to empty their pockets, but these were the sort of cruel people for whom a hundred coins is just the beginning. For the most part, people's hearts in this world of ours are all pretty much the same.

The Starshine teahouse in Akenogahara is an exceptionally amusing place. At any time of the year the tea ladies are all elegantly dressed in tea-leaf print kimonos with red linings. Moreover, nowhere else in all of Japan do the ladies put on their makeup as thickly as they do here. Local tastes are, after all, local tastes, and regional preferences are always catered to, an Ise man's bulrush being an Osaka man's reed; even the famous Sumiyoshi teahouse cannot enforce uniformity in the appearance of the tea ladies at its branch shops around the country. Not surprisingly, then, most of the travelers from afar who stopped at the Starshine teahouse did so not to flirt with the ladies but to enjoy a moment's respite from their journeys.

Now in this area with its fields of sacred pines were two singing nuns who for the past thirty-four or -five years had made their living entertaining travelers and pilgrims with songs as well as other favors of a more personal nature. The people in these parts had given them nicknames, and called one Grubby Insect Jurin and the other Old Badger Seishun; every last packhorse driver and palanquin bearer knew them by reputation. When they were not singing they would approach the travelers, look them over, and say, "Hello, you fellows from Matsuyama in Iyo," or "Welcome, dear monk from the Shoshazan in Harima," or "Greetings to the lady from Okayama in Bizen," and ninety-nine times out of a hundred they would be right on the mark.

Once a vacationing man was passing through on a tour of various temples and invited the two singing nuns to join him at the teahouse. "No matter how practiced you may be at this craft of yours, I find the matter just a bit too remarkable," he said to them. Then he challenged, "So let's see if you can tell me where I come from and what I do for a living."

"Well, you look like a Chinaman, but our guess is that you're from Nagasaki," one replied.

"How could you know that!" the man exclaimed. "Is it the way I look or does my speech give it away?"

"Well, everything about your speech says that you're from Izumo, but those two men you have traveling with you both speak with Nagasaki accents. You look to be about fifty-five or fifty-six years old, wear white satin underwear, and have a telltale patterned velvet-collar which, together with your gold long sword, suggests that you're a man of some means. You *are* from Nagasaki, aren't you?"

"I was sent to Izumo while still a boy to be adopted by a family there," the man explained, his interest now all the more aroused, "but a chance to return home to Nagasaki luckily came up, and that's what brings me here. Well, you've done quite well so far, but how about telling me what I do for a living?"

"That might be more difficult. You see, there are some complications."

"You'd better tell me," he said, and so they continued.

"Please forgive us for saying so, but don't you have some connection with the licensed quarters? When we first looked into your eyes a moment ago we thought we saw some sort of intimate association between you and a beautiful girl not yet fifteen years old, but it wasn't love of a physical sort."

The man was absolutely astonished when he heard this, and with tears streaming down his face he said, "It's an embarrassing little portrait you've drawn of me. But I swear to you by the Sun Goddess Amaterasu herself that I have never been a brothel keeper. The beautiful girl you saw in your vision is actually my daughter. Some twist of karma from a former incarnation may be responsible, but she's thirteen years old now and still can't stand up properly, and what's more she's disfigured with something called Turtle Belly.* On top of all this she's blind in both eyes, and I dare not broach the subject of her marital prospects. Many are the days I've spent weeping, because whenever I see a girl of about the same age all I can do is think, 'If only she were like that.'" His tears did not seem at all out of place.

Just then there came along a strikingly beautiful woman of some twenty-two years who looked like a lady of the Capital. She was riding in a hired palanquin as was her traveling companion, a rather dandyish-looking clerk. The two singing nuns went running over to them and said, "Hello there, honored guests from the Capital. We've been sitting here all spring and no couple as handsome as you has passed our way."

The young man, with a gleam in his eye, said something like, "Small world, isn't it?" and handed them each a few *momme* before passing on.

The man from Nagasaki asked the nuns, "Just who were those people?"

"Well, from her looks you might guess she's a tea lady from Gion or Yasaka," they explained, "but she's really a married woman just dressing the part. That clerk she's with is using the pretext of a pilgrimage to Ise with a baser target in mind."

Just as they finished speaking, a matronly sort in her middle thirties straggled over to the teahouse and sat down. The man from Nagasaki asked her what she knew about the palanquins which had just gone by, and she volunteered,

* Abdominal dropsy.

"Those good-for-nothings? Every time they stop at an inn on this Grand Shrine visit of theirs, they make 'pillow talk' till dawn. The two of them have planned it out so that, by sending their bearers on instead from some place called Obata, they won't actually have to visit the shrine. The woman is married, and the clerk talked her into sneaking off on this trip without asking her family's permission. If word were to reach his employer of just what he's doing, he'd dismiss him in a minute. By chance I wound up being employed by the same people, but though my feet hurt terribly, they just drove on ahead and never offered to let me ride along with them." She said all this with considerable malice, and then walked on by herself.

The next people to come by were three men, each of whom had a *furoshiki* bundle slung over his shoulder. The nuns came up and said, "Spare us a copper?"

"We'll give you some on our way back," they said.

"But you won't be coming back this way."

"How can you know that?" they exclaimed.

"You're only passing by the shrines. You're really craftsmen on your way to Edo to earn some money."

The three men stopped dead in their tracks and said, "We'd like to hear how you know all this."

"Since you only came here on impulse when you got to the Suzuka checking station, your loincloths are ragged. What's more, all three of you have souvenir fans from the Tokaido highway, which means it must be your first trip to Edo."* The men were all astonished and moved on without looking back.

---

* The Tokaido was the most important of the five major highways that linked Edo with the rest of the realm. Between Edo and the cities of Kyoto and Osaka along the Tokaido there were numerous checking stations *(seki)* where officials examined travelers' papers and belongings.

Just then there came along a strikingly beautiful woman of some twenty-two years who looked like a lady of the Capital. She was riding in a hired palanquin as was her traveling companion, a rather dandyish-looking clerk. The two singing nuns went running over to them and said, "Hello there, honored guests from the Capital. We've been sitting here all spring

and no couple as handsome as you has passed our way." The young man, with a gleam in his eye, said something like, "Small world, isn't it?" and handed them each a few momme before passing on. The man from Nagasaki asked the nuns, "Just who were those people?"

TWO: PEOPLE'S HEARTS · **177**

Some time later a group of respectable-looking men came along. "And where are they from?" asked the man from Nagasaki.

"Those are Nara men on their way to the shrines, and they may all look like distinguished men, but they're watching every penny on this expedition. No matter what we say to them we won't coax more than one *mon* out of that bunch."

Just as they had predicted, their purser came following behind and from a string of cash he untied a single copper *mon*, which he handed over for the two to share between them. Still standing there, he pulled a portable pen-and-ink case from his pocket and in his petty-cash account book he recorded the words: "At the Starshine teahouse the singing nuns approached us and noisily made various demands to the effect that we give them seven or eight pieces of silver. Having no alternative, we duly . . ." This is the very height of pedantry.

The next group to come along was composed of four young men, each with his hair tied in a fashionable topknot, each possessed of a kind of reckless gaiety, and each quite obviously infatuated with the dyed pattern on his summer *yukata*. They approached the teahouse in a way that suggested the journey was very much on their minds.

"And who might they be?" asked our Nagasaki friend.

"They're from the seaside at Otsu. . . ," replied the nuns and by the time they finished they were already half-way up to the men to solicit a contribution.

The young men made various pointless requests to the nuns, such as asking them to sing songs or describe famous sights in the area, and when they were finished they said, "Now as you nuns know by looking at our faces, we're going off to the Ishiyama Temple, and if you want anything from us you'll have to come and get it," and with these words they all ran off.

"Hey! Wait a minute," the nuns cried after them.

"Maybe fate will have our paths cross again," was their only reply, and by then they were already out of sight.

The nuns had a good laugh and said, "Look, one of them dropped his pocket mirror. If we call them back maybe they can spare us a copper in exchange! That Ise Shrine certainly doesn't waste time in punishing a thief when it finds one!" And they chatted on with our old friend from Nagasaki, but eventually he too had to go off on his way.

"Haven't you left anything behind? Now, don't forget anything. . . ."

•17• The buddha box that no one saw for free

Inside the Monjudo Temple at Kireto in Tango Province there is a statue of Kindoji.* In order to have the curtain behind which it stands drawn, all would-be worshipers are required to pay a fixed fee of one hundred *mon*.

Now in the arms of this Kindoji has been placed an object known as the Wisdom Box. Foolish pilgrims believe that if they pray to the statue the wisdom of the Buddha will be imparted to them, but the fact is that the ignorance you are born with will never be transformed into the wisdom of Manjushri. Should you ever be shown this so-called Wisdom Box, you will see for yourself that it is an ordinary strongbox like that in the home of any merchant.

The real lesson of this statue is that each day of the year you must make a faithful record of your financial transactions. I have yet to see the man who can record entries in his ledger any which way or ignore details in his calculations

* One of two attendants to Manjushri, the Buddhist God of Wisdom.

and still make a successful living. A person guilty of this kind of sloppiness feels that there is no lasting glory in living to be a hundred years old. By his way of thinking, only a fool would waste his time on thoughts of his descendants in a world that one knows but briefly, and that being born with good fortune should suffice to get a man through life. But since he reckons that even if a person inherits a considerable sum of money from his parents he can still end up a pauper, he lives by tiding himself over one day at a time and never worries about what the future may hold in store. When this kind of irresponsible parent leaves his children a predictable pile of debts, they, in turn, grow into parents who spare no amount of work and labor in building their own homes. From the iron bucket in the stone wellcrib to the copper gutters on the eaves, and even to the household furnishings, each of their bequests to future generations represents the fulfillment of a life dream, and each hands over a cash box sealed intact. These two sets of parents are as different as can be.

Some time ago there lived two elderly, wealthy, and happily retired gentlemen from the town of Sakai in Izumi Province. They had been friends for many years, and one year while making a sightseeing trip to view the pine trees at Amanohashidate they stopped along the way at this Monjudo Temple. They carefully considered having the curtain drawn back but decided that the one hundred *mon* required to see the Wisdom Box was needed for more immediate expenses and that not paying out this money would be a supreme sign of the gift of wisdom; so they left the temple without praying to the statue. These gentlemen were fine parents who used every opportunity to economize. Thus they had good livelihoods, and they never neglected even the most trifling detail.

Some time ago there lived two elderly, wealthy, and happily retired gentlemen from the town of Sakai in Izumi Province. They had been friends for many years, and one year while making a sightseeing trip to view the pine trees at Amanohashidate they stopped along the way at this Monjudo Temple. They carefully considered having the curtain drawn back but decided that the one

hundred mon required to see the Wisdom Box was needed for more immediate expenses and that not paying out this money would be a supreme sign of the gift of wisdom; so they left the temple without praying to the statue. . . . "The best place to pray for a long life or for the success of your livelihood is right here at home."

Now the children of these gentlemen announced to their fathers one day that they wished to visit the Taga Daimyojin Shrine in Omi Province in order to pray for long lives, but their fathers were quick to point out, among other things, the utter uselessness of making such a pilgrimage.

"There is no need to call on the help of the gods. If a person wishes to prolong his life, he should avoid wenching and drinking; in a world with delicacies like cedar-grilled foods, he should give up the abalone broth and avoid the company of those whose means are above his own; he should stay out no later than his neighbors, get up earlier than average, and never be careless with family business; even if there is some tempting offer of quick and easy profit, he ought never to leap into speculative ventures outside his own field.

"He should let his abacus be his friend and comfort morning, noon, and night, and he should make the holiday settling of accounts his first priority. There is nothing quite as injurious to one's prospects for old age as borrowing something and then having its owner come pressing for its return.

"As proof of this advice, there is a man who often accompanies us on our temple visits. He had two daughters, one sixteen years old and the other fourteen. As befits a well-to-do family, nothing was overlooked in the preparations for his daughters' marriages. He provided each with the most beautiful clothing and dowries of one thousand *chokin*, and he married each one off to a son-in-law of the kind he had hoped to find. Since the elder sister's family steadily prospered, she prospered, too, and stayed young and pretty; the glowing appearance she had as a bride is still with her even now that she's over thirty. People nicknamed her the Female Immortal and said, 'Now here's someone to envy.'

"This woman never drank from a fountain of youth or ate

mermaid flesh, but she did eat yellowtail fish when they were fresh after the tenth month. She always finished her New Year's preparations during the eleventh month, and this year she again saw the blossoms of another fifty *kamme* in her account. She only listened to good news and treated her eyes to joyous sights, and by living her life in this way, she shows not one sign of having aged.

"But her younger sister, who is not even thirty, already looks seven years older than her older sister and, sad to say, has lost her former charm. At one time she was regarded as both the more beautiful and more lively of the two, but as her domestic circumstances fell upon hard times she did, too, and became thoroughly disagreeable. She ate whitebait and octopus until the end of the third month, well beyond their season, and was depressed by the lack of household funds year after year. Even the disposition of her husband changed from the old days, and he would suddenly become enraged over the least little thing. Thinking that because she was married her most important concern should be the declining fortune of her family, she sought various ways to improve her husband's spirits and tried her hand at menial work like washing and pressing silk. If the two of them went sightseeing or flower viewing, she resented the expense of hiring men for the carriage and developed imaginary ailments when there was nothing wrong with her.

"As a matter of course she became withdrawn around others at family functions, and even in her speech she would follow another's lead. And also quite naturally she began to pay less and less attention to her personal appearance, which became quite untidy. At some point she stopped wearing short-sleeved long kimonos and slipped into wearing narrower sashes. It was sad the way her emotions aged her.

"Generally speaking a woman and her husband are drawn along by the fortunes of their households, and in this sense we can say that a person's appearance is artificial. Now the fact that this older sister should both look younger and cling to life more than her little sister is all due to the encouragement she received from the prosperity of her family. So we tell you that you should devote yourselves to working hard in life rather then waste your time praying to out-of-the-way gods and Buddhas."

This was the advice of a knowledgeable elder. His friend continued: "No matter which doctor's hands you put your trust in, a human life has a limit to it, and no matter which gods you put your faith in, there is no way they can help you to live a single day longer. The best medicine for helping you reach a ripe old age is working hard at your living before your forties so that you can sit back and enjoy life after the age of fifty. You can pray to Taga Daimyojin, and you can trek off to distant parts of Omi, but if you stop and dally along the way back at the Shimabara licensed quarters in the Capital, then you'll run head-on into the God of Poverty. The best place to pray for a long life or for the success of your livelihood is right here at home." Thus spoke a man who overlooked nothing.

Nowadays one can see any number of people whose expressions suggest that they are enraptured with thoughts of the hereafter, but genuinely devoted people are rare. Everyone is concerned with his own fame or prestige. To their parish temples people donate wall tiles emblazoned with the family crest, or on the path to a temple they construct footbridges marked with their surnames. In any event, the primary motive here is to make the parishioner's name known to the world. If a man's real intentions are toward the hereafter, then he should make a point of not having his name and address entered into the parish registry each time he gives rice to some poor priest.

These days not a single soul seems bent upon living the Buddhist life. When it comes to making their livings and dealing with people, all these priests are not the least bit different from lay persons. Excluding those temples with large endowments, however, one cannot criticize the way priests curry the favor of a potential benefactor, however unbecoming such behavior may be. They actually have no alternative.

If the abbot of a temple gets up to dance in the middle of a banquet but admits quite frankly, "When your stomach gets used to austerities, that wine can take a heavy toll," people will like him and say, "That abbot's all right." But if a priest walks around constantly fingering his rosary beads and having nothing to say to the pilgrims except a ten-fold chant of the Buddha's name, then laudable though he may be as a priest, no one will give him a second thought.

It is especially amusing to have a look at the new-style monasteries with which priests are now affiliated. Every day in Higashi-Kozu the priests manufacture a special kind of thin makeup powder; in Shiomachi the nuns are continually busy making scarlet satin loincloths; in Nagacho the priests sell fishhooks; in a hermitage in Dotombori the clergy produce sharp metal prongs that are used like barbed-wire on the tops of fences or walls to discourage burglars; in Tamazukuri the priests make their living by being professional go-betweens all year round; and in the Teno Temple, the priests make money by hiring out mendicant's robes on a daily basis. Then there are the bonzes near Fujinotani who make short-term ten-day loans and devote all their spiritual energies morning, noon, and night to the intricacies of calculations on the abacus.

Now although these men might have shaved heads, walk in dark priests' robes, and look like real holy men, deep down inside them there beats the heart of a fiend. They ring their bells and recite their devotional prayers, but that is not the only way they make their livings. If it appears that temples everywhere are growing more and more gaudy and are dazzling in all their brilliant splendor, this is not because the Holy Buddha has been so effective in bringing people into the fold. It is due to the efforts of some abbot wise in the ways of the world.

• 18 • Spending a day at the employment agency

"The months drift by as quickly as the waters of the Asuka River,"* almost as if in a dream. This spring a worker was hired for six months by a bedding manufacturer and, before he knew it, the fifth day of the ninth month arrived and he was once again out of a job. The story of those special employment agencies for half-year working men and women has all sorts of amusing aspects.

Sometimes I wonder just who was the wise man who came up with the idea of hiring people on a six-month basis. For the woman of the house it is a clever arrangement, since if the employee does not suit her husband's fancy she knows that the term of employment is only for half a year. For the most part the situation can be tolerated until a new servant with a fresh face arrives, at which time the old one can then be given her notice.

But the system also has advantages for the employee, since if she should be hired by an especially heartless employer,

---
* An allusion to a poem from the *Kokinshu*.

she can still make it through the days since it is only for six months. Then, after finishing breakfast on the appointed day, she can quickly put her personal effects in order and cheerfully wear a smile.

"No matter where my next assignment will take me, I would be ever so grateful if from time to time you kindly think back to the period I spent in your service. Miss Nurse, I grilled those mushrooms you asked me to pick this morning and put them in a colander, which you can find shelved inside the cupboard. Also, those metal chopsticks which were misplaced? Well, I noticed them stuck between two *tatami* mats in the parlor and put them in the silverware box for you. If the man from the beauty parlor comes by with my hair cream, excuse me for all the trouble but could you please pay him these thirty-two *mon*? Also if the lady from the cleaner's arrives with the dyed cotton I ordered some time ago, please have her drop it off for me.

"I'll stop by in another four or five days to pay my respects. As for all you houseboys, now if we should meet on the street, you mustn't pretend that you don't recognize me any more. Kyuza, if we meet around here in the rain, I hope you'll have the good manners to loan me your umbrella. Finally, I sincerely hope that the girl who takes my place will be agreeable to you." So with these few reminiscences and not a little nostalgia for old times, she sets off for her new job.

Now since servant girls invariably come from vulgar classes, there are no problems involving loss of face when one wishes to discharge them. All one has to say is, "The family has asked me to inform you that your contract with us has expired, and though I dislike the prospect of losing you, my hands are tied; so I must ask you, such a dear, sensitive girl, to leave."

For her part, the girl understands that she has displeased her employer. "I'm certain that this will be all for the better," she says, and like the water thrush that leaves no muddy eddies behind, she washes out the jars and puts in fresh water before taking her leave.

But there are also times when the woman of the house has a wretched disposition and finds fault with the most impossibly trivial things. She attacks the servant by complaining to her daughter-in-law: "That girl we hired for the summer term let all the rice boil over onto the floor, and then I saw her walking about crying in the rain, her head wrapped in her apron. But I've heard that the harvest was bad in Harima this autumn and girls from there who are just the right age are sure to come begging to be employed in exchange for room and board. Where else could you find a girl who can not only boil rice properly, but also weave, operate a husking machine, baby-sit, or even chop wood? Take that girl of ours who's tasted work all over Osaka, that saucy little wench whose right hand is blistered from holding a ladle in it all her life—no one is going to employ her. She'll have to sell that one kimono of hers just to get enough to eat, and she'll wind up a streetwalker strutting about humming her little ditties."

When the woman finishes delivering her tirade, the servant girl, who is not about to stand by silently, goes over to the sooty kitchen cat and prods its ears with a poker, saying, "You're supposed to use your ears, too, so whether you like it or not, listen to what I have to say. The only reason we feed you and let you play all year long is because we expect you to catch mice. So long as you don't run off with the dried bonito, there's nothing in the world for you to fear. After all, no one says you have to sleep under this caldron.

"If you're annoying the master and he throws you around

Now since servant girls invariably come from vulgar classes, there are no problems involving loss of face when one wishes to discharge them. All one has to say is, "The family has asked me to inform you that your contract with us has expired, and though I dislike the prospect of losing you, my hands are tied; so I must ask you, such a dear, sensitive girl, to leave." For

her part, the girl understands that she has displeased her employer. "I'm certain that this will be all for the better," she says, and like the water thrush that leaves no muddy eddies behind, she washes out the jars and puts in fresh water before taking her leave.

or hits you, you can always run off to some mansion in Kitahama or Nakanoshima where they entertain guests every day and never take out the garbage. They'll give you the leftover goose and carp entrails.

"You know, you agreed to come here without requiring new clothing and to work for room and board alone, but if it's fish you want, why, when they buy a box of eighty dried mackerel and grill it for supper, they'll let you sniff all you like. Who advised you to come here, anyway? If you stop to think about the thousands of nice homes where you could live just as easily, I guess you're not that lucky after all," says the servant girl by way of returning the attack, and from then on not a day goes by without the family and the girl snarling at each other.

The woman of the house grows increasingly furious with the girl and says, "A person can never win against masters or illnesses, so from now on, whether you like it or not, you're going to get up before dawn and you're going to polish that caldron and mince those dried greens. You're well cut out for the work of a scullery maid. Now get to work on that hole in the mosquito netting!"

The girl just answers her, "Even if I only work here one day more, I'd prefer it if you kept your finger on my nose and made sure that you got your money's worth out of me. As long as I'm working, you'll be pleased!"

From then on, the girl leaves a trail of destruction behind her. The large pot has cracks in it; not one of the set of ten serving trays is left in its original condition; the neck of the vinegar bottle is broken off; the edging on the nested boxes is peeled away; the parasol lies hidden under the floor boards; sandals are thrown on the roof of the bathhouse; and she manages to cause who knows what other damage to her employer's possessions. It is a fact of life that the lower classes are vulgar, and it is the mark of a clever woman when she knows how to manage her servants.

One indication of the hard times on which we have fallen is the enormous number of women who are looking for half-year employment this spring. A first-class servant who is perfectly suited for the kitchen of some prominent family and who before could have expected to get forty-five to fifty *momme* for six months' work, can at best get only forty *momme* this year; the salaries drop even more for servants with lesser credentials. An above-average girl who could have fetched thirty *momme* is now hired for as little as twenty-five, and one below her who formerly earned about twenty-two *momme* now has to settle for eighteen. Some frail young girl good for sewing and weaving who might have earned fifteen *momme* will not get more than one *kammon*; as for her clothing benefits, she will have to settle for just one hempen unlined summer kimono, if that.

One of the conditions under which these girls now work is that the semiannual allowance for cosmetics and rouges or for buying sandals will become their own expense from this year on. When one of them is out of work and is living in the employment agency's hostel, she pays the daily room and board charge of two quarts of rice, rain or shine, and as the days add up she resorts to selling her own clothing just to stay alive. When she does find a place to work, her hostel expenses are deducted from the advance on her wages, and then the employment agency deducts its ten percent commission. Such servants end up going to work with only the clothes on their backs, but I have yet to hear of a servant going naked to her new job.

Even if no one offers a girl a job and she becomes like a masterless samurai, she clings to her one fashionably printed kimono, her wide silk sash, her one pair of cotton split-toed socks, and her silk floss veil and ornamental comb, for these things are as important to her as the long and short swords are to a samurai; she would rather go without food for three days and drop dead than part with a single one of these items.

While the life of a servant in a hostel can be oppressive, even servants with long-standing jobs sometimes intentionally return to their old hostels. If you ask such a woman what she hopes to gain by this, you will discover that her goal is surprisingly trivial. It is not that she means to derive pleasure from indulging in an act of seeming madness. Rather, since she knows that women always envy a beautiful lady dressed in the latest fashions, she wants only to have everyone's eyes on her when she walks into the employment agency with her hair elaborately done up and the nose on her particularly flat face held high in the air.

For this occasion, one of these women put on the special Yang Kuei-fei* makeup for the first time, thus fulfilling a lifelong dream, and even smeared her face with rouge. Then with mincing steps and a straight back she self-consciously sashayed into the hostel as if it were one of the world's grand boulevards. Most people would have been embarrassed to be seen like that, but the attitude of this one was "Never mind."

Of course to the temple disciple, the craft apprentice, the widowed traveling salesman, and the country boatsman, this woman presented a view different from what they could see in the countryside, and they intently directed their gazes on her hips as if to drill right through them. Regarding their attentions as one of the pleasures of the Floating World, she continued to walk through the town day after

---

*Yang Kuei-fei was a Chinese of legendary beauty.

day; to her way of thinking, surely no one would have given her such looks unless she were genuinely attractive. On all her jaunts through the city, however, not a single soul followed her back to the agency or was love-struck by her, and after a while her self-confidence was plagued with doubts.

"The world is full of blind people," she thought to herself. "It seemed, to me at least, that compared with the appearance of the other women who made the equinoctial temple-visit today, mine was not at all third rate; yet there must be something wrong if no one's falling in love with me!" She took out her pocket mirror and, putting on a smile, she looked at herself, first holding the mirror sideways and then rightside up. But during this one-woman show, while she was checking her features very carefully, she noticed her feet and was disgusted by the fact that they were so large that even a man's socks were too small.

"Perhaps this dates back to when I was two or three years old and accidentally stepped on the wand used at the Great Purification Ceremony, or to when I stepped on the charm for the god Nio. People say always leave three inches for doubt, but when a woman has feet four inches wider than average, it's no wonder men are uninterested. If a woman has just one flaw that draws attention to her, it spells sadness and loneliness."

One evening this woman was leaning on the arm of a lonely widower whose collar was dirty. "It's a bad sign for a man to wear clothes like that when there's someone who'd like to wash them for him."

"I'd like a thoughtful woman like that," he replied.

"If only you'd be patient with me, I'd love to do it," and seizing the opportunity she asked, "Are you free tonight?"

The man considered her offer for a moment and said,

"Let's get some sakè and have some fun, and perhaps I can get you to give me a backrub."

"Oh how embarrassing, but it must be my fate to be so madly in love with you. Just lead the way!"

The man stood up to go home, but then took one step back. "If these things aren't straight right at the beginning, there's always trouble later. If you-know-what happens, will you take responsibility for the midwife expenses?" he whispered.

Somehow or other, you know for certain that this woman, too, will be forsaken by the God of Marriage. When a woman peels off every little bit of discolored skin to make herself more attractive, a man won't mind paying her lodging expenses or giving her a little extra spending money; but even in this world where a woman can always put the pinch on a man, there are definite exceptions to the rule.

Considering how much things cost these days, you just have to stop and wonder at certain women. You should have seen the pair of ladies I saw stroll into the agency. Their salaries were fixed at fifty *momme* for a six-month period, but incredible as it seems, one of them was wearing pure white *habutae* silk from the Capital with a red-checkered lining from the Omori boutique and a China-tea-brown satin sash. And if you looked further, you would see that she had a long, gaily patterned gossamer slip, a translucent tortoise-shell ornamental comb, a rainbow-patterned undergirdle, and who knows what other accessories. A rough estimate would be that she was wearing at least two hundred and seventy *momme* worth of outfit. The dutiful clerks at the employment agency just had to question her as to how she had managed this from a fifty-*momme* salary.

This woman's companion went up to the front desk and said: "If there is an opening for my friend, we must get a few things settled before she can take the position. First, she must have six evenings a month off to observe the fasts—religious reasons, you know. Then she expects to have two afternoons off each month. Also she needs the six holidays for the patron of travelers, and she must have free the evenings of the eighth and twenty-second of each month for observances to the Yakushi Buddha, as well as the twenty-fifth day of each month for prayers to Lord Michizane. Finally, she never does housework between sunset and eight P.M."

"And is it thanks to her devout spirit that she can afford these clothes?" queried the man behind the desk.

Realizing that he must be on to their game, they turned on their heels and walked softly off into the distance chanting, "*Namu Amida Butsu,* all praise be unto you, oh Buddha . . ."

• 19 • A pawn ticket for a set of armor, with headpiece

The town of Fushimi down alongside the Capital, with the single exception of its main boulevard, now has a lonely and desolate air. The sadness of things there is especially evident in the autumn, the time of year when tea masters once plucked blossoming morning glories from hedges and fence rows for use in the tea ceremony; these days no one pays much attention to the old ceremonies, and the bucket from the well lies in disarray, entangled in its own rope.

The petals of the bush clover form a brocade for no one to see, and on the branches of the hibiscus are hung out to dry the diapers of some crying infant. Even the Matsudaira compound, where in long gone days men and their ladies would while away the days of spring, is now a thinned-out vegetable garden; where banks once lined the broad avenues, there is not a single home left that gives the appearance of having a hundred coppers.

The place is barren except for the odd shop selling oil

for three *mon* or salt for one *mon,* and the only time of year when one can find even salted sardines is around New Year's Eve.

Because it is only two miles from the Capital, even a woman could stroll there after supper and still be back in Fushimi at a respectable hour. But those now in Fushimi are ensnared by their poverty and most of the women and children have not even seen the face of the Capital's Great Buddha.* Off to the east and deep in the mountains lie the remains of Fushimi Castle, and the swarms of people who go there hunting for mushrooms are not out for their own amusement but just for filling orders from the green-grocers on Second Avenue. Even catching and selling insects becomes a makeshift way for these people to make a living.

When you examine this town with its thousands of families struggling by whatever means they can find to get by in the world, it is hard to believe that the small dock on the Yodo River once helped pull them through and enabled them to put food on the stove morning and night. Back then, these people grasped firmly the oars of their livelihoods and rode roughshod through the annual waves of uncertainty.

Placing one's articles into hock is an activity by no means limited to poor people and is a recourse to which most anyone will turn when faced with straitened circumstances. In former times the Sen-no-Rikyu school of flower arrangement placed the esoteric Maeoki arrangement of the *Iris Japonica* into hock for one hundred *ryo*. Likewise the Hananomoto school of linked verse pawned the word "dew" for one hundred and fifty *ryo*. The hearts of people in the Capital are truly extraordinary, for taking a man's pledge as his word,

---

* A statue in the Hoko Temple on Seventh Avenue in the southern part of Kyoto.

they will lend money without insisting upon a guarantor or upon fixing a terminal date for repayment.

But as things work out, when a person's things are in hock—the flower arranger deprived of his *Iris Japonica* or the linked-verse poet denied the word "dew"—he finds the terms constricting, and the pledges are paid. There was an impoverished courtier who, lacking anything substantial to pawn, hocked in exchange for one *kamme* his most cherished possession—his Kakinomoto Hitomaro ancient-style beard, perhaps the only thing in which he genuinely took pride. The terms of the agreement were biannually renewable and stipulated that at the end of each six-month period he had to come to the pawn shop equipped with his razor and shave off whatever growth he might have acquired during the interim. He racked his brain to find a way to pay the original loan plus the accrued interest in order to retrieve the rights to his beard.

Similarly, there is the amusing story of the courtesan in the Shumoku licensed quarters who, finding herself pressed for cash, actually placed one of her love letters into hock. The proprietor of the pawn shop considered the matter carefully and loaned her cash in exchange for the letter, assuming that while the courtesan was saving up money from the hands of her patrons, the loan could be accumulating interest. This "love letter," however, was not written out of any overwhelming sense of affection; rather, it read, "As my life as a courtesan has fallen on hard times, I hereby reveal to you the true state of my circumstances. For many years I have gratefully received your secret patronage, and in return for that support I have kept our matters strictly confidential and treated you with tenderness. If my intentions should ever change, may the gods bring their wrath upon me and may I sink to the level of some five-*fun* whore."

The sadness of things there is especially evident in the autumn, the time of year when tea masters once plucked blossoming morning glories from hedges and fence rows for use in the tea ceremony; these days no one pays much attention to the old ceremonies, and the bucket from the well lies in disarray, entangled in its own rope.

The pawnbroker made her write this utterly fallacious document and even went so far as to have her apply her personal seal to it in blood. Furthermore, by exchanging one-half *ryo* for each such testimonial, he eventually managed to count among his customers courtesans ranging from the high-ranking *tenjin* down to the common prostitute. This scheme had been devised by a salesman of hair ointments who often passed through the licensed quarters and who himself had managed to make quite a tidy profit from it without anyone suspecting a thing. Since the girls knew that in the event they were unable to repay the loan the pawnbroker could show their letters to people and claim that he was their secret lover—which would mark the end of their livelihoods—they always kept to the terms of the agreement and not once did he suffer a loss from these ventures.

There is nothing in this world quite as cold-hearted as a pawn shop. It is an enterprise definitely not meant for anyone with a weak stomach. Especially in a pawn shop will you find every manner of pitiful soul, people who live only for the day and have no idea of what tomorrow may bring.

Pawn shops, no matter where they are, close during the day and do most of their business in the evening hours. On one particularly cold evening with a pouring rain and howling gusts of wind, a man in his forties using a cushion for an umbrella walked into a pawn shop and took off the only piece of clothing he had on, an old cotton jacket for which he received, after the necessary negotiations, one *momme* and seven *fun*. After wrapping the coins in his sash, he walked out the door stark naked except for a simple loincloth.

On another occasion, an old woman in her seventies, hanging on to her cane every inch of the way, tottered into the unfloored entrance of the pawn shop and from inside the folds of her kimono pulled two antique mosquito-net hangers from the Higashiyama period.

"It's too much trouble to draw up a pawn ticket for something this small," said the proprietor as he handed her sixteen *mon*.

"Can't you at least spare twenty for them?" implored the old woman, clasping her hands, but it became apparent that it was not to be. "There's no use in staying here any longer," said the woman, and taking the few coins in her hand, she went shivering and hobbling out the door, where she fell over and died. Since people who frequent pawn shops are poor, the proprietors never think of these incidents as particularly upsetting.

Another incident occurred when a ship was making its way down the Yodo River en route to Osaka. The men on board often disembark at Fushimi to hawk pulverized burdock, a local specialty, and one of them came to the shop with a full set of braided, ancient-style armor, headpiece included, which he claimed had been used in the Battle of Sekigahara. The proprietor saw things somewhat differently, however.

"This hardly looks like it belongs to you," said the proprietor. "Sorry, but I can't use it."

"But I'm trying to pawn this for someone else," said the man.

"That's all very well and fine, but you just bring in something that looks like it might be yours and I'll think about it."

Just then the door opened and a man with his hair tied in a bundle at the nape of his neck stuck his flustered face through the crack and said, "All right, Proprietor, that's my set of armor, if you must know, but under no circumstances can a samurai's armor be taken from his own hands and pawned. Actually, I'm willing to act as guarantor for the transaction, so it shouldn't matter to you if even a woman came here. That headpiece is especially interesting, for it was originally given to Minamoto Yorimitsu near the Hachiman Shrine to use in the Battle of Oeyama. It's a real treasure."

"In that case, it is all the more hard to handle," said the shop owner. "Perhaps you could rent it to a temple as a religious property."

"Why, that's ridiculous. So this is not as pawnable as some ordinary cotton jacket?" lamented the samurai, and he picked up the armor and walked out the door.

A gentleman told me the story of the difficulties this masterless samurai encountered while attempting to make his living in the merchant quarter of town. The same gentleman informed me that, as a rule, it is a mistake in judgment for people who have fallen on hard times to use a pawn shop. These people may borrow one hundred *me* against their possessions, but when the interest charges are added on there is no way for them to raise enough money to get their articles out of hock. In most cases, he advised, it is preferable to sell your things right away for whatever you can get for them.

The man also said that he himself had placed things in hock on more than fifty separate occasions but had never managed to get a single one back from the pawn shop. After going through all this, he realized that if he had pawned seven articles one at a time instead of all of them at once, he would have had seven pawn slips, each one of small denomination. The chance for getting any one item back would then have been far greater.

It is just too hectic to pawn your mosquito netting in winter and bedclothes in summer. It is a cheerless life when you time and again pawn the formal clothes you need on holidays. No matter how humble a household one might have, any man who aspires to being a gentleman would do well to realize that there are certain articles of clothing—jackets, suits, and short swords—that are appropriate to certain occasions. Since these things are requisites for the merchant, he would be wise not to part with them, even if it means skipping a meal now and then. It is simply impossible for a merchant not to attend such affairs as wedding receptions or the funeral of an associate. Domestic finances are his wife's responsibility, and she must instinctively present her spouse in the best possible light.

There was a man from the wholesaler's neighborhood who put his wife's entire trousseau, including fashionably tailored clothing, bed clothes, bedding, and even household utensils into hock. Against all this he was able to borrow seven *kamme*. When people inquired into what he was doing, they learned that, just as they might have guessed, his bride had come from the wealthy town of Uji and that before twenty days had passed after the wedding reception he had already borrowed his wife's clothing and deposited it securely in the storehouse of one of the local pawnbrokers.

The only way he had been able to get this bride in the first place was by fooling everyone into thinking that he was a man of some substance, and the woman was disconsolate when she realized just what had become of the man on whom she was to rely for the rest of her days. Actually, when you stop to think about it, this kind of shameful situation in life is invariably the consequence of people trying to make themselves appear better than they are.

In this instance the proprietor of that pawn shop also met a bad end. He had become quite wealthy over the years and had been all too quick to forget the harder side of life. At one point, he took to wearing a fancy pongee uniform and to renovating his old shop—replacing the shingles on the roof with new tiles, washing the walls, and installing grating. His new house glared out in run-down Fushimi, and poor people, naturally, felt ashamed to even approach it. Before long he had no customers. Eventually his capital dwindled to the point where he had to change his store into an oil and rice shop, and in the end he was forced to sell the house outright.

For those of you who are thinking of running a pawn shop for a living, never even consider the notion of renovating your old house. Do not permit your wife to wear fancy short-sleeved kimonos; take every precaution against fire in the storehouse; and try to get a fierce-looking, wise old tomcat, one that will make a good mouser. Finally, you should think of your abacus as your only child and cradle it in your arms when you go to sleep.

•20• A lady's change of heart

A man wise in the ways of the world once said, "One thing that holds true in this world is that we shall always be plagued with rats by night and thieves by day, so be forewarned!" But assuming that you *are* this careful and consider every last detail, does this mean that you should never light a flame in your cottage or set foot in a seafaring vessel? Not really, for as far as human beings are concerned, their fates lie in the hands of Heaven.

They say that even if you are struck by a bolt of lightning, your death has been preordained by your actions in a previous incarnation. Be that as it may, it is the lot of most people to die a natural death after having lived a full life in which they were prudent and used every opportunity to avoid personal danger. Accordingly, many daimyo and members of the nobility have hired carpenters to construct what they call "earthquake-lightning" rooms in their homes. They use copper shingles on the third story, stretch special curtains over the ceilings, hang hollyhock from the Kamo Shrine in each of the corners, and burn exotic incenses alongside the drapes.

As soon as the first lightning flashes are spotted, the mistress of the house proceeds to the shelter, where she is surrounded by ladies-in-waiting who press into the room and recite relevant passages from the *Kannon Sutra,* and time after time the danger passes without incident.

Be that as it may, high-born people pile up their brocade cushions all they want, but there is no escaping the shadow of death, just as there is no way to decline the offer when the Buddha's launch comes beckoning to you. When you stop to think about it, it is difficult for a person to be very cautious about his appointed hour. People are all too quick to ignore the matter of their death; they while away the months and years engaged in the pleasures of the flesh.

This is especially true of girls employed in the homes of prominent families. These girls are quite often the daughters of relatively well bred people. From their youth on, these girls have no idea of the unpleasant aspects of life in this world, and exclusively for the sake of deportment they receive training in the correct behavior of ladies at the court. All day long they lose themselves in playing the lyre and reading poetry. Their lives are made up of flowers at dawn and snow in the evening, of full moons and autumn colors; but what they really long for is love.

In a world divided between sex and strong drink, they make themselves as attractive as possible, and in this half-dreamlike state, they experience neither sins nor sorrows. Just as "To know the source, one must drink the waters," these girls never encounter poor people from humbler stations and the harshness of life in these times is completely foreign to them. Accordingly, they never acquire the economy-minded spirit of a woman who will wear gaiters so as not to spoil the hem of her kimono.

But let me tell you the story of a young woman named

Lady Nightingale who worked in a personal capacity for one of the more distinguished families. On the twenty-fourth day of the first month, a time when the plum trees were in bloom, her employer requested that she visit the Kitano Shrine on his behalf. On her way home the streets looked peculiarly unfamiliar, but from the scene outside the window of her carriage she realized that she was passing the small-looking houses of the Nishijin part of town. All of a sudden the gentleman with her recalled that at the shrine he had forgotten to leave the donation separate from the fee for the Kagura dances. Flushed with confusion, he dashed back to the shrine saying, "Wait here a moment."

Lady Nightingale had the carriage stop by a gate from behind which could be heard the sound of a loom, and there she rested under the eaves of the house. She heard the sound inside of an earthenware mortar, and she saw that since the scullery maid was busily working away, the still-young wife of the master was able to sit for a spell and, with her beautiful hands, select greens to use with the rice cakes made from the New Year's leftovers. All this was just to please her husband, who, happily stretched out, was using the doorsill as a pillow and reflecting on how easily his household had made it through the recent holidays.

"It must be hard," he mused, "for courtiers to get dressed up and put on those hats, and daimyo must hate wearing ceremonial gear with those swords dangling at their sides. I tell you there's no life as good as a merchant's life. I've read a poem that says, 'You went into fields to pick herbs for your lord . . .,'* but if it were me I'd have said, 'When a man has his wife select greens for him . . .,' for that's the better fortune of a busy kitchen."

* From the *Kokinshu* anthology.

She was incapable of managing worldly matters, no matter how trivial, and since her beautiful appearance alone was not sufficient, she was divorced and sent home. Later Lady Nightingale married the owner of a cosmetics shop on Fourth Avenue. He used her as a kind of walking advertisement, but here, too, she was unable to deliver a proper sales presentation. Again she was put out

the door. One humiliation was heaped upon another until she had no sense of shame left. . . . A person who knew Lady Nightingale both before and after her escapades said, "It applies in reverse to men, too, but a woman must never, ever long for a husband whose family background will prevent him from understanding her own."

"Ah, now that's the good life," thought Lady Nightingale as she perked up her ears and wholeheartedly envied the scene before her. Even after she returned home she did not forget it, and, pleading the excuse of illness, she asked for permission to leave her duties. Some time later her curiosity drove her to marry a merchant, but what her husband found simply intolerable was the way she found it so terribly amusing to turn rice into rice cakes, or her amazement that a flame should burn by oil instead of wax. Similarly, she was incapable of managing worldly matters, no matter how trivial, and since her beautiful appearance alone was not sufficient, she was divorced and sent home.

Later Lady Nightingale married the owner of a cosmetics shop on Fourth Avenue. He used her as a kind of walking advertisement, but here, too, she was unable to deliver a proper sales presentation. Again she was put out the door. One humiliation was heaped upon another until she had no sense of shame left and wound up married to an entertainer who worked the teahouses in Higashi-kawara. At first his family employed a servant girl, but declining finances later forced Lady Nightingale to handle the household responsibilities alone. Since their livelihood consisted of whatever they managed to receive from the hands of others, there were only disappointments. They resorted to buying on credit throughout the year without ever paying off their debts, and her husband was never at home during the holidays.

At this point Lady Nightingale was at her lowest, and her former appearance was gone. She wore an old light blue kimono with patches sewn onto the right sleeve to shield herself from the icy gusts of the eleventh month, she used twisted paper string for a sash, and she would not even arrange her hair into a simple chignon. Since she did not even bathe once every twenty days, her skin acquired the texture of a caterpillar's, and she neither trimmed her nails nor applied tooth black. When you add her shrill voice and her infernal squawking, well, who could have imagined that she would sink so low?

Hand in hand with this, her disposition sank to fearfully dismal straits, until she had no qualms left about walking by herself late at night. If some stranger approached her, she was of a mind to use the opportunity to coax some money out of him, and by becoming expert at twisting the words of bill collectors, she gained a new name for herself: the Lady Swindler.

She turned to repairing split-toe moccasins by the piece as well as to making twisted-paper hairbows, stitching tobacco pouches and woven sashes, wrapping incense sticks, and so on, but instead of doing the work and returning the articles to their owners, she would invariably take the things and sell them to buy food. She thus managed to keep herself alive for eight or nine years. Rumors spread to the effect that, "You'd better not trust that woman," but the size of the Capital enabled her to make it through the year by means of these swindles. Not even her patron saint could have guessed that she would turn out this way.

People's hearts change with the times, and there is just no telling when good times will turn to bad. If you keep this in mind, you can see that the only reason she threw away her undeserved life in service to a nobleman was that she envied an ineffectual life in the home of some merchant. A person who knew Lady Nightingale both before and after her escapades said, "It applies in reverse to men, too, but a woman must never, ever long for a husband whose family background will prevent him from understanding her own."

•21• A few words on servants

"We're housemaids," announced the two girls as they walked together into the employment agency, but since the going wage for a housemaid was everywhere fixed at sixty *momme* per six-month term, their prospective employer made no attempt to bargain and simply looked them over to decide which one would better serve his needs. After all, since the duties of a housemaid are primarily to wear a short-sleeved uniform, to accompany the mistress of the house in her carriage, and to act as a messenger on formal occasions, she should know how to deliver long verbal messages, and when her mistress has guests, she must be able to prepare light refreshments, keep the trays well supplied, and make certain that the kitchen and its adjoining rooms remain spotless. She performs exactly the same functions as what is known in samurai families as the "tea girl." These girls are simply indispensable, and every home needs at least one to look after all the whatnots.

Now of the two housemaids I mentioned, one was not at

all attractive. Her face was completely ordinary, with the exception of her front teeth, which protruded in a most disagreeable fashion. The second girl, on the other hand, was of just the right age and thoroughly qualified for the job, and any family would be more than grateful to have such a splendid addition to its home.

In order to help the employer decide which one to hire, it was agreed that each girl would go and work in the house for one night on a trial basis. The less attractive one went first, and it was discovered that besides her ability to perform all the tasks expected of a housemaid she was so skilled in writing that she could easily pass for a private secretary. "I should like to please you by playing the lyre," she said, "and I can also work a loom to make pongee for you." The more one asked of her, the more cheerful she became, and having her employed in the home would be a great asset.

When it came time for the second girl, the prettier of the two, to have her try, they learned that she was slightly deaf in her left ear and did not even know how to play cards when asked to be a partner. In fact she was so incompetent that when she saw a washbasin with handles on each side she had to ask what it was. When the family delved more deeply into her record, they were shocked to learn that she was prone to epileptic seizures two or three times a month.

You can never tell about people just by looking at them. After this girl was fired, the madam of the employment agency whispered to the master of the house, "Listen, as long as she's good-looking enough, I can always sell her to a teahouse for one year and make one *kamme* and four or five hundred *momme* on her."

"It's a fact of life in this world of ours," replied the master, "that good things never come in pairs," and the whole matter ended with a hearty chuckle.

People say it's unfortunate that you can never know what a person is really like. In former times a girl not yet in her teens whose features were not unwholesome could be hired as a parlor maid, but nowadays when townsmen are more aware of their own interests, girls in their twenties are hired and are expected to do the work of ten people by themselves. These girls are thoroughly capable of making their own way in the world, but because they have been unable to marry into an appropriate household they are hired on contracts for as long as five years, with seasonal bonuses of silk clothing and an advance of only one hundred *momme* against their wages. They are drawn into a life in service with a view to the future and often take up with one of the clerks or other servants, their main wish being to make their prospects for the future as secure as possible.

But there are also girls who look just like any other parlor maid but whose intentions are quite another matter. These stylish women, who fabricate as trustworthy an impression as possible, are actually parlor thieves. At first they show themselves to be simple and naive homespun types, and cultivate the favor of their mistresses. Once one of these girls has become sufficiently friendly with her mistress, she will turn to the master.

"I know how to cut and arrange hair," the girl offers one day.

"That'll be most appreciated when we're short of hands."

Then, on a day after being summoned to give the master a trim and shave, she snuggles up against his back under the pretext of having made a mistake, and as she picks up a clump of hair from the floor, her hand slips inside his kimono onto his neck. After stroking him here and there, without any bidding on his part, she proceeds to slide her hand inside the broad opening of his sleeve. Sensuously grinding her hips in rhythm with her stroking, she succeeds in arousing her master's passions, and pretending that she is beside herself with her own passionate longings, she painfully pinches the master in his ribs.

"Not so hard!" he cries.

But as she withdraws her hand, she whispers to him so as not to be overheard, "Look, it's your wife!"

"Just be still, my pretty little one," he says playfully. But this is just the start of their playing, and eventually she makes herself available for his pleasure on two or three more occasions.

Then one day she says, "Oh, for some bitter plums!" and it is no ordinary whim of the stomach. "You'd better think of something before your family finds out."

She threatens the master with blackmail and uses every opportunity to look queasy, placing the master in an awful bind. Her next step is to inform her parents, who then contact the master in strictest confidence and instruct him to pay five *ryo* or seven *ryo*, or as much as ten *ryo* if his circumstances permit, as a payoff for their silence. And only then is he free to dismiss her and conclude this ugly affair.

Yet another variation on this theme is for the girl to say, "Just look at my condition. And what about your wife? Why just think what your associates might say. If my father were to catch word of it, well, he didn't raise me to end up like this. There's no point in my going on in this world. I shall throw myself into a river." This is another way to threaten money out of an employer. When a father and daughter team up, they can extort money all year long. A woman who would make a desirable parlor maid for some man because of her good looks will make inquiries to locate an especially wealthy family whose master has a weakness for women.

She will announce her willingness to work for just room and board and some small presents of clothing. This kind of woman is a real scoundrel.

"Therefore, any man who considers the tenderness of matrimonial vows or the grief his wife would feel or what people would think or any of the other ramifications of such affairs, will not even for a moment entertain the notion of getting involved with one of his servants," or at least these are the words left to us by a man with good sense, a man who learned his lessons first hand and later took those lessons to heart.

It is part of the human condition that no one keeps his head when it comes to children. No matter how stupid a child may be, never say a harsh word about him in front of his parents. Even if we see the dissuading stick being raised over a child who has repeatedly been bad, we feel a bit sad when no one appears to smooth out the situation before it's too late.

When the lad is under the age of seven and, for example, takes chopsticks in his left hand or smashes the tea kettle with a hammer, you should make a special effort to say gently, "A strong spirit like that, now that's the mark of a man! Later on he'll hold those chopsticks in his right hand like us!" Likewise it will not do for you to praise the intelligence of one child in front of another's parents. If someone else's child has just finished reading the *Great Learning** at the age of five, they won't hear a word of it, but if their own child should, at the age of eleven, pick up a broom and pretend to be a spear carrier, the parents will commend his

---

* The *Great Learning*, traditionally attributed to Confucius, was used throughout East Asia as a primer for teaching children to read Chinese characters. It is, nonetheless, a difficult text.

grip and have the boy repeat his act whenever there is company. Now it is easy enough to laugh at these things when they are other people's affairs, but if you yourself should ever become a parent, each stupid little thing your foolish child does will, to your eyes, appear very clever.

Children from the lower classes are invariably dull and undisciplined because their mothers do not raise them conscientiously. By the time they are three years old, they have already acquired a sense of cunning that they will not lose should they live to be eighty. Common country folk would really like to entrust the upbringing of their children to wet nurses but the chain of expenses involved obviously puts it beyond the means of such middle- and lower-class people to hire one. By the time her salary of eighty *momme* and her clothing expenses—including formal and informal sashes, pocket handkerchiefs, socks, and gloves—are totaled up, even a wet nurse working for one of the lesser families will cost three hundred and forty-five *momme* a year. This explains why the children are nursed by their own mothers.

An average girl married at about age seventeen and for the first year or so she dressed herself up as prettily as if she were going cherry-blossom or wisteria viewing. As far as her husband was concerned, so long as his wife looked like that he would happily put up with it. At mealtimes she would even daintily decline to eat the leftovers of the elegant sidedishes she had prepared for her husband. But when that first child was born and she had to wash and dry the diapers with her own hands while the stench overpowered her, she no longer thought of the child as something to delight her in her old age.

"What kind of karma brought this on me?" she complained uselessly, and from then on she gave up on life and even stopped going to the theater and visiting the Teno

Temple. Finally, since the family was not earning enough money to provide well for the child, they placed it in the hands of their only housemaid, though they then resented seeing her step out with their child's diaper bag hanging from her arm. It is extraordinary how strange a woman can become in this world when her heart is taken over by pride.

The real uncertainty in life is death. There are women who become seriously ill after giving birth and who die leaving behind their only child as a kind of memorial, and while they are safely on the road to the hereafter, their husbands experience a grief more severe than any other in this world. If the husband is a man who has no difficulty in making a living, however, he can always, for the right price, hand the child over for adoption by some childless family or make inquiries to locate a wet nurse so that his child will receive constant care and attention.

But the torment of one impoverished widower was that each time his child cried, he lost his spirit and recalled his wife's dying expression and the words she had repeated to the very end: "It's too awful. Please think of the child as if it were me; don't abandon it." Before three days passed, he had decided that despite the hardship, he could not hand over the child to anyone else, much less dispose of it under some footbridge. He was determined that as long as he was physically able, he would raise his son to be a man. This proves that there is still a sense of right and wrong left in the hearts of people in this world.

Since the child was still too young to eat powdered baby food, he was obliged to find real mother's milk. During the daytime, people who were aware of his misfortune helped him get milk for the baby; but when he tried knocking on a neighbor's door one night after the ten-P.M. bell had tolled, it was quite a different story.

If their own child should . . . pick up a broom and pretend to be a spear carrier, the parents will commend his grip and have the boy repeat his act whenever there is company. Now it is easy enough to laugh at these things . . . but if you yourself should ever become a parent, each stupid little thing your foolish child does will, to your eyes, appear very clever.

"Have you all gone to bed already?" he asked, uttering a prayer. "Are you all asleep?" he tried again, repeating his prayer, but there was still no answer. "Since there's no way to keep you alive, my son," he cried out in a last desperate attempt, "will your father have to wrap you up and drop you off the Naniwa Bridge?"

This time a voice came from inside the house. "I've spent the entire day ginning cotton and rashly thought I might get a bit of sleep."

"I know it's a bother, but can I just have a word with you?" he importuned, holding out the baby.

"We weren't able to buy lantern oil tonight," and as the voice trailed off, so did the light from the lantern and all was in darkness.

He got it into his head that no matter how old this woman was, he somehow might succeed with her husband away, and so on that frosty evening he stood in her gateway and used various forms of flattery and cajoling such as, "It's only a minute of your kind time for which I ask." He went home to bring back a cup of oil, but first lit his own lantern and spun cotton for a while in his workroom—it really is a disgrace for a man to do women's work.

Since the baby cried when he tried to take it back later, he changed his mind about trying to find milk that evening and then spent another sleepless night waiting for the dawn, when he would have to get up and spend yet another day washing diapers and hanging them out to dry.

The next morning he presented the woman with a gift of some dried fish on a platter, feeling all the while confused and upset. Such a life can do horrible things to a man's heart. For a man to be poor and at the same time try to raise an infant without mother's milk is the root of much sadness in this world.

• 22 • A parent's love for his child

Even among townsmen, the birth of a child into a prosperous family is a preordained event. The life of such a child will be intimately tied to the realm of worldly affairs. His parents even hire both a wet nurse and a nanny, but only after having thoroughly scrutinized their family histories. Then they place them under the supervision of one of their most trusted senior servants.

The nurse and the nanny may not go off, even briefly, for a rendezvous at the employment agency hostel, nor may they sport hairpins or berets. They are made to wear silky fabrics next to their skins, and their meals consist of porridge in the mornings and flying fish and sconders as well as other foods in a balanced diet. At night they post a sleepless watch at the foot of the child's bed, keeping a close count of how often he dirties his diapers. Three times a day they give the infant a solution of five exotic incenses, and the family physician makes an uninterrupted stream of housecalls. One could go on and on about all the attention lavished on such a child.

People say that the three greatest scoundrels are packhorse drivers, ship's captains, and wet nurses, but a wealthy family expects its nurse to be thoroughly qualified and will not delay a single day in firing the woman if she displays any personal interest that might even slightly interfere with her care of the child. The nurses know and fear this, and dare not utter a sulky word or demonstrate that the young master is not their primary concern.

A substantial number of the women working as nurses today are of two types. The first woman is a victim of a broken home. The second is a woman who, lacking a proper husband of her own, grew restless for a man's company, was forced to hand the child of that union over to some employment agency hostel, and is still now producing milk. She seeks employment as a wet nurse even though she has only the most naive notion of how to raise a child.

After entrusting her case to the madam of the agency, she is assigned as a child's personal nurse until he reaches the age of five, though she has no idea what the protocol is when the child receives a present of a helmet in the fifth month or a toy bow in the first month or when she herself gets gifts from her employer. From the ceremony of the First Haircut to the First Wearing of adult clothing,* she receives gifts of silk clothing to mark the occasions, but she carries on working oblivious to the significance of the events. She is just not suited to being a wet nurse.

One of the most troublesome aspects of hiring a wet nurse is that she will try out various schemes in order to perform another year of service. She saves up her milk for two or three days, borrows someone else's baby, and then, clutch-

---

* In the eleventh month of the child's fourth year and first month of his fifth, respectively. These mark the end of the nurse's service.

ing the child close to her with the most sullen expression on her face, she goes to the house of some family with a young child and says to the lady of the house, "I've just given birth and the curse is still with me," as if she were just some amateur at all this. Then she bares her breasts and squeezes out a few drops to show the woman. "I had some words with the baby's father just four or five days ago," she continues, "and I've been so sick with worry that I haven't eaten a thing since then and I can't feed my baby." She delivers these lines without so much as a twitch of the nose.

"Calm down and have something to eat—that milk will come again. Your little baby's a girl, isn't she? We have a little boy here and I'm certain they'd get along just fine," says the woman, unaware of the ruse to which she is about to fall victim. They draw up her contract and let her borrow her entire salary in advance. Meanwhile, all night long their precious child is forced to lap at the inadequate supply of milk.

"I can't understand what's wrong," says the child's mother, examining the situation.

"Well, it's because I'm not really related to your baby," explains the nurse. "Since my milk won't gush out like a waterfall, I think it would be for the best if you hired a new nurse. I've already given the money you loaned me to my ex-husband to have divorce papers drawn up. . . ." she rattles on with her fabrications—causing all sorts of trouble and using the same tricks over and over again on dozens of families. But the madam from the employment agency who conspires with her is just as guilty.

Truly there is nothing in this world as heartrending as the plight of a woman whose family life has ended in divorce and who, with nowhere else to turn, allows her husband to convince her to become a wet nurse. Though relations between a husband and wife may be thoroughly bad and each year grow worse, even if they agree to get a divorce they will still have feelings for each other. Ask any man and he will tell you the same story.

Even if they are poor, a husband and wife can have fun in talking things over, and as the days turn into months and the months into years, a blessed event will take place, and they will have a child. However this will mark the end of their fun, for they will soon discover that because of the baby they can never hope to make ends meet.

Time after time one such couple made secret plans to join hands and jump headfirst into a well after stabbing the child to death. But each day they put off their plans, and after a time the child was able to put its own hand to its mouth and make a smiling face. This made the old grannies from the neighborhood come to play with the baby and praise him to the skies. "Just look at those earlobes! That's a mark of good fortune, and those are lucky bright eyes if I ever saw them." The parents then started to think that even if they should both die, the baby, at least, would have a chance of making it in the world.

One day they broke up the offerings tray for firewood, boiled up some water, and realized that this was all they had left to live on. The baby then began an unprecedented, continual flow of cries, and when the neighbors came in to see what was the matter they were shocked to learn of the true circumstances of this family.

"How could you have kept this from us for so long?" they exclaimed. "Since you're perfectly capable of producing a fine lot of milk, why don't you work as a wet nurse for one of the better families, and with the money you earn you can have your baby raised as a foster child. As long as a husband

and wife have not changed their basic feelings for one another, once they've had a chance to get back on their feet they can learn to live with each other again."

"You're so right. Let's give it a try," they replied. Surrounded by the bustling of the valiant old grannies, they located both an employment agency for the woman and a family into which the baby could be adopted, and in just over four hours the couple was well on its way to a new life. In due course, with Osaka being such a large place, they were able to learn a new degree of freedom.

Over time, the husband and the woman with whom he had shared his life until that morning, found their evenings lonely and full of remorse over being separated from their dear little child. With the money left over after paying the foster parents for the baby's upbringing, the husband used three hundred and seventy *mon* as capital to begin supporting himself cutting tobacco leaves.

Now in general, from the moment a bride and groom exchange vows, they reckon their expenses with the assumption that a child is to be included among them. No matter how poor a family may be and no matter what kind of tiny hut they live in while they make their way through the world by taking each day as it comes, once their child is safely born they have to allow five gallons of rice and eight hundred *mon* for delivery expenses. Because this particular husband never really understood what having a baby involved, he was consigned to live the rest of his days in a solitary, lonely existence.

•23• Some advice for when you make your fortune

Any businessman who struggles year after year to make his financial roots more secure and stable can be said to grow rich in much the same way that the camphor tree grows tall—slowly but with a firm base. Whenever he rode into battle, the great warrior Kusunoki Masashige always carried a special banner on which were written the following five words: injustice, principle, law, authority, heaven. Kusunoki's way of life was to stress righteousness and belittle death, and the meaning of these five words was that injustice must yield to principle, principle to law, and law to authority, with authority being ultimately subordinate to the will of Heaven. Time and time again Kusunoki manifested these truths in his battles, and not once did he fail to win the just cause.

Every human being must learn the secrets of his trade, as it were, from the family into which he is born. This is true, for everyone, be he samurai, farmer, craftsman, or merchant. A man should not allow himself to become foolishly contemptuous of the trade that devolves upon him before he has even left the womb. If we look at people's hearts in this world of ours, however, we can see that a young man inherits a tiny rice shop from his parents but, disliking the dust and the pounding noise of hulling, he switches to the stationery business, and once he is in the stationery business he longs to open up a dry goods store; eventually, by always wanting things which look good from the outside, he ends up losing all his original estate.

In commercial ventures it is an infallible rule that the businessman well versed in the ways of his trade will succeed in making a living. Nevertheless, the major difference with times past is that we have entered an age where only money makes more money—a period in which the average man with a bit of money stands a better chance of making a profit than does the man who uses all the wit and ingenuity at his disposal.

Now in the Capital along Muromachi Avenue, among those heads of famous families whose houses line the long boulevard there is not a single one who is incompetent in his way of making a living. And all who work there, from the managers down to the junior clerks, are well accustomed to life in the midtown of the Capital and are quick to hear of any rumor or gossip making the rounds. They are good judges of a man's character and have learned the fine points of a hundred and one trades without any outside instruction. A man's character does seem to depend a great deal on where he makes his home.

It is quite amazing how different the people of the Capital can be. An apprentice in a needle shop in Anegakoji labored ceaselessly throughout the year, busily working his awl to open eyes in the needles and cut them to uniform length. He knew nothing of the cherry blossoms at the Ninna Temple, or of the autumnal foliage beside the Tsuten Bridge. He never even witnessed the spectacle of Mountain Floats in the Gion Festival on the seventh day of the sixth month, and his only pleasure from the occasion was the welcome opportunity to eat holiday noodles and fish salad.

But there was another young man of about the same age who worked for a very prominent family. To him the fourteenth of the month meant that girls of the Gion licensed quarter had the day off, and he would make a date with one of them at a house of assignation, arrange to spend the day in revelry at a tea house, or secretly rendezvous with a bathhouse whore and pass the day with her watching the Mountain Floats from a rented one-mat box in the reviewing stands.

There was a clerk still in his internship who squandered his pot of gold every which way and spent an enormous amount of money. But another fellow in the same outfit who was never short of money in his purse would say, "Even if I could make two or three hundred *me* in my private ventures, it still wouldn't be enough for me to strike out on my own." He also threw away his money on all sorts of useless things.

The conscientious assistant in the needle shop was once sent on an errand to his employer's wife's home town, where he was to deliver some holiday presents. As a tip for his service he received ten *mon* for each of the presents. He saved up the tips, and his only thought was, "Now I've got one *momme* eight *fun!* All my life I've wanted a narrow red loincloth, and now I'll have it." There is nothing in this world as varied as human beings.

If you were to inquire into just what it is that makes a family become wealthy, you would find that it is the diligent efforts of the family's trusty employees. Likewise if you were to look into the reasons why a prosperous family should suddenly lose its fortune, you would find that they once again hinge on the nature of its workers. In former times it was the practice to make profits by virtue of the conscientious efforts of one's staff, but nowadays it seems the rule that money spent on clerks is just wasted. It is due to the bad judgment of the employer that so much of his money falls into others' hands. If an employer does not make the necessary inspections when account books are put in order and instead spends his days in sightseeing, in playing in the licensed quarters, or in lazing around on boats, oblivious to the New Year closing in upon him at such a fearful pace, and if he does not even examine his financial drafts and relies entirely on the judgment of his clerks, then whenever his clerks tell him to affix his seal upon a document he will open his case as if in a dream and sign whatever they put before him.

"Thanks to the extensiveness of my markets in this world, one press of my seal is enough to open doors worth one thousand *kamme*," one such man senselessly boasted to his new bride. The gentleman endowed with the ownership of this business was not content to confine his activities to making a living for himself, and by virtue of his kindly disposition, he allowed countless people outside his immediate family to rejoice in making their livings through him—there is no greater way to serve one's fellow man.

In former times, even if a man only did a complete accounting twice a year, at the Festival of All Souls and at New Year's, he would always perform the chore most carefully. Since he examined the accounts at the end of each month, it was impossible for there to be even the slightest degree of falsification—the clerks being so busily scrupulous. Of course they had no time for private ventures, being, quite understandably, so absorbed in the affairs of their employer,

It is due to the bad judgment of the employer that so much of his money falls into others' hands. . . . Whenever his clerks tell him to affix his seal . . . he will open his case as if in a dream and sign whatever they put before him. "Thanks to the extensiveness of my markets in this world, one press of my seal is enough to open doors worth one thousand kamme," one such man

senselessly boasted to his new bride. The gentleman endowed with the ownership of this business was not content to confine his activities to making a living for himself, and by virtue of his kindly disposition, he allowed countless people outside his immediate family to rejoice in making their livings through him—there is no greater way to serve one's fellow man.

and they worked conscientiously and blamelessly, for they knew that his gain would be their own.

Nowadays it is very important that an employer himself do all the negotiations directly with the people to whom he plans to loan money so as to have first-hand knowledge of what they are like. In the society around us it so often appears that when an employer is prospering, his employees will compete with each other to be first in his eyes. They can be most diligent in seeing that the employer continues to turn a profit, but if his circumstances are on the wane, they will not think of making one great effort to help pull the business out of rough times. Rather, they arrogantly feel that since this venture will not last much longer, they need not bother with it, and this attitude will simply hasten the firm's bankruptcy. In any case, when dealing with your subordinates, you can safely say that everything hinges upon just how well you manage them.

There was once a man who set himself up in business doing exactly what he pleased and made the sum of one thousand *kamme* by the time he was fifty-three years old. But in that year he took seriously ill, and as the end drew near, he called his son, who was nineteen, close to him and said, "After I'm gone, you must not engage in this business under any circumstances. If you try your hand at it, the money will all be gone within ten years. Be a money lender, only don't let out a mortgage unless the value of the house is at least ten *kamme*." He had his employees accept various presents of money, and just when the business was at the peak of its prosperity, all activity came to a halt, and the estate passed into the hands of his son.

Although some people regretted that this family should discontinue its business, they realized that everything had gone according to the wishes of a man who had turned a paltry sum of money into a fortune worth one thousand *kamme*. When they saw what became of the family, they realized that in the son's hands this had become the kind of happy household with so much money that the only problem was finding a place to put it.

◆ ◆ ◆ Suggestions for Further Reading

Two good books that will give readers of Saikaku some insight into the life and literature of the Edo period are Howard Hibbett's *The Floating World in Japanese Fiction* (New York: Oxford University Press, 1959) and Donald Keene's *World Within Walls* (New York: Holt, Rinehart and Winston, 1976). Keene's book includes an exceptionally informative chapter on Saikaku in which references to the present work, *Saikaku Oritome* (Keene translates the title as *Saikaku's Last Weaving*), can be found on pages 206–10.

Some Saikaku translations are *Five Women Who Loved Love*, translated by Wm. Theodore de Bary (Tokyo: Tuttle, 1956); *The Japanese Family Storehouse*, translated by G. W. Sargent (Cambridge, Eng.: Cambridge University Press, 1959); *The Life of an Amorous Man*, translated by Kengi Hamada (Tokyo: Tuttle, 1963); *The Life of an Amorous Woman*, translated by Ivan Morris (New York: New Directions, 1963); "Saikaku's Parting Gift," translated by Robert Leutner in *Monumenta Nipponica* 30 (1975), pp. 357–91; *This Scheming World*, translated by Masanori Takatsuka and David C. Stubbs (Tokyo: Tuttle, 1965); and *Worldly Mental Calculations*, translated by Ben Befu (Berkeley: University of California Press, 1976).

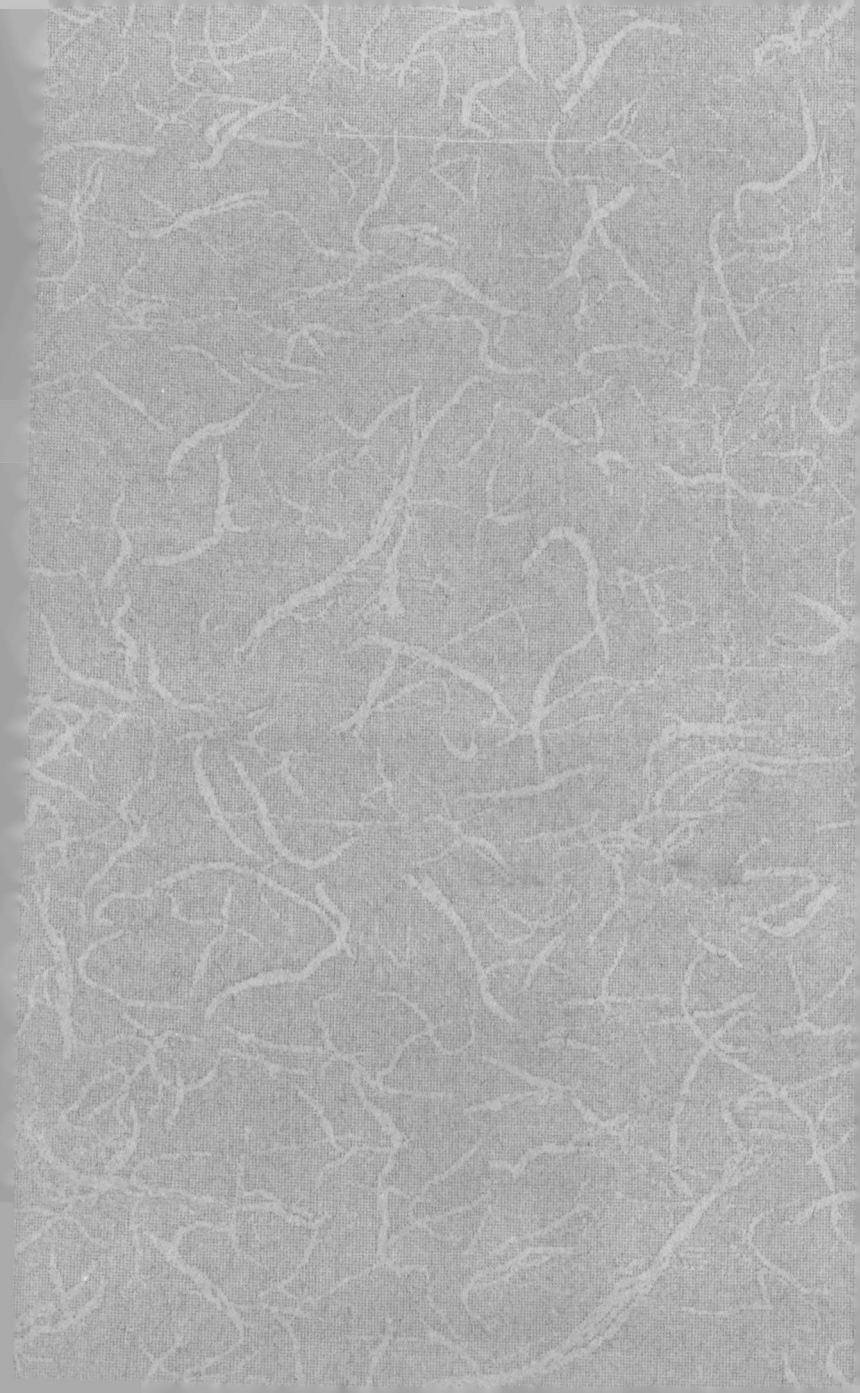

895.633 IHARA
Ihara, Saikaku, 1642-1693.
Some final words of advice
$12.00

MARICOPA COUNTY LIBRARY DISTRICT
3375 WEST DURANGO
PHOENIX, ARIZONA 85009

© THE BAKER & TAYLOR CO.